THE
HARVEST
EATING
COOKBOOK

MORE THAN 200 RECIPES FOR
COOKING WITH SEASONAL LOCAL INGREDIENTS

BY CHEF KEITH SNOW

PHOTOGRAPHY BY TRAVIS RUNION

RUNNING PRESS
PHILADELPHIA · LONDON

∾

To my brother, Steven,
who has been a tireless supporter of Harvest Eating.
Our Harvest Eating victory is as much yours as mine.

∾

Library of Congress Control Number:2009928393
ISBN 978-0-7624-3741-2

Cover and Interior design by Amanda Richmond
Edited by Geoffrey Stone
Typography: Berkeley Book, Helvetica, and Italia
Food styling by Keith Snow, Patrick Hartnett, and Tia Maria Bednar

Running Press Book Publishers
2300 Chestnut Street
Philadelphia, PA 19103-4371

Visit us on the web!
www.runningpresscooks.com

TABLE OF CONTENTS

ACKNOWLEDGMENTS

I AM VERY HUMBLED TO HAVE HAD THE opportunity to write this book. There are many people to thank. First and foremost, my editor for putting up with my missed deadlines and my sometimes poorly organized work, thanks Geoff! Patrick (Patty-Choux), who jumped in with no life vest to help organize my jumbled mess of a book, you rock man! Those close friends and family members whose prayers, monetary support, and encouragement helped keep Harvest Eating alive during many lean financial years when it seemed just a money pit and an impossible dream. My own family, especially my incredibly lovely wife Sonja, for continuing to believe in me and help support my dreams which oftentimes seemed unlikely to come true. My amazing children—Olivia Rose, Ava Elizabeth, and soon to be born Garrett Peter, who are a daily inspiration for me to continue modeling the traditional farming lifestyle, while trying my best to provide healthy food for their enjoyment and nourishment. Thanks, Mom (and Dad) for cooking delicious foods (especially soups and eggplant parmesan) and helping make food the main event in my life. Thanks to my in-laws, Elisabeth and Mike, your food traditions and recipes are gifts that keep giving and will always be cherished by our family and our viewers. Special thanks to the talented team at Harvest Eating who care tremendously about the mission we're on to change people's eating habits through exciting, well-crafted visual media. Joseph and Travis, thanks guys, it's been a great ride! I'm grateful to the loyal Harvest Eating fans and viewers who have supported me with kind words, well wishes, and detailed feedback throughout the years. I especially want to thank God for giving me the ability, desire, and raw ingredients to create great food, and the tenacity and focus to make this adventure become a career.

INTRODUCTION

MY LIFE'S CULINARY JOURNEY

I GREW UP IN NORTHERN NEW JERSEY in a small town; it was suburbia, a great place to grow up. My days as a young boy were very typical, nothing out of the ordinary. I have very early memories of the foods we ate and how my parents loved good food. There were many amazing meals, especially at holiday dinners. I clearly remember those tables set with fine silver and adorned with linens, candles and of course, great food. We had perfectly roasted turkeys, hams, and roasts all served with plenty of delicious vegetable side dishes. I loved the sausage and apple stuffing, green beans, mashed potatoes, baked sweet potatoes, Brussels sprouts gratinée, asparagus, broccoli, steamed cabbage and much, much more. The desserts were equally memorable.

This constant culture of great food shaped my taste buds and my future pursuits, even though I had no idea it was happening. During this time I remember cooking with my mother in the kitchen, licking spoons and whisks filled with freshly whipped cream. These experiences helped shape my love of food.

I vividly remember trips to Van Riper's Farm and Tice's Farm, two vibrant small farms and markets in suburban New Jersey, and weekend trips to the family's farms. Both of my uncles (on Dad's side) we're involved in farming. There were dairy farms in upstate NY, the other near the Amish country in Pennsylvania. In addition, my oldest uncle raised award-winning Morgan show horses in New Jersey. The time spent at farms helped fuel my love for the farming lifestyle. Those fond memories led me to purchase land and build my own farmhouse and horse barn when I returned to the East Coast to raise my family. I have raised chickens, dairy goats, and still keep Paso Fino show horses on the farm. I often say "I was born to be a farmer, but wound up a chef instead."

Then it happened, in 1981, at the age of fourteen, a good friend asked me to help him by taking over his dishwashing job at a local Italian restaurant for one weekend so he could vacation with his family. I sheepishly agreed to help, but, to be honest, work was something I was not used to. I'll admit that being the youngest of four kids, I had an easy time around the house. I really did not do any chores whatsoever, this included yard work, which my older brothers took care of. So, at the age of fourteen I ventured into the kitchen of a busy restaurant as a shy, 110-pound kid with zero work ethic.

Chef Phillip Pelicano the owner was a gracious, fiery yet kind man who helped me to quickly learn the business of scrubbing pots and pans, plates, cups, bowls, and silverware. There was no dish washing machine. Each piece was washed by hand, every knife, fork, and spoon. I can remember struggling to keep up during the busy hours when the plates were quickly moving out to the dining room and coming back twice as fast. I remember furiously scrubbing dinner platters for the chef when he had only one or two left in his stack with ten dishes of food on the stove yet to be plated.

Eventually, I managed to keep up and also found that the happenings at the stove and in the pizza oven were far more interesting to me than the dishes I was cleaning. I think my boss, a hard-working retired Italian Navy chef, could see that I loved food. I loved eating it, prepping it, smelling it, and just being around it. Chef Pelicano was like a second father figure to me and treated me with a fondness not usually experienced at work, certainly not in a professional kitchen.

His food was simple, consistent, and delicious. I can still remember the taste of his food: the melted cheese, tangy tomato sauces, buttery shrimp, and amazing thin crust pizzas. Those initial food experiences solidified my love of food, my love of cooking, and my future. Of course I did not know that until twenty-five years later.

Fast-forward eleven years to 1992. With several more cooking gigs under my belt including stints in California and Florida, my desire to diversify in the food industry led me to create a brand of Italian-inspired food products—pasta sauces to be exact. I created four distinct flavors of all-natural pasta sauces and managed to have them distributed all across the country. This was no easy task, breaking into the food products industry took lots of money, experience, and contacts, of which I had very little. During that time I was still working in professional kitchens in Florida. Eventually, I left the kitchen to focus on the growing food products business. It was a wild ride and a great learning experience. I was often at the receiving end of tough business lessons taught by wily food industry veterans. About eight years later, having worked myself senseless, I found myself back in the kitchen of a small restaurant on a part time basis. I was now a married man. At that point I realized that I loved the food much more than the grind of the commercial kitchen. I needed to be around food, but not shoveling it through the service window of another lousy restaurant. Maybe the management side of kitchens would serve me better? This question led me to take the executive chef position at a busy Rocky Mountain ski resort. It was a fast-paced busy resort with multiple food outlets: catering, coffee shops, and a general store of sorts. This was a chance to work with some great people and gain some invaluable work experience not to mention enjoying the outdoors as well.

During those Colorado years our family expanded with the birth of our first daughter, Olivia Rose Snow, who was one of the catalysts for my current endeavors. I realized what a blessing a child is and the awesome responsibility raising one can be. When Olivia was just about ready to start eating solid food, about six-months-old or so, my wife and I started discussing the future of Olivia's diet. I had never thought about it before and quickly realized that these decisions would affect her health and well being throughout her lifetime, not to mention her relationship with food. We decided that feeding her with natural foods, organic when possible, would be the best choice. We made all of her baby food from scratch and kept her diet perfectly clean for years to come. This meant dealing with lots of fresh vegetables, food mills, juicers, strainers, and other tools and methods of making baby food. We didn't feed her any jarred food or bottled juice whatsoever—just fruits and vegetables, organic hand-ground grains that were crafted into cereals and of course lots of Mama's milk.

Now, I am the first to admit that my wife had more to do with this than I did. She is a very determined, take-charge gal that has discipline akin to Chef Pelicano, however she is much prettier. At this point in time I had virtually no exposure to organic foods. In the restaurant business, only a select few were sourcing organics and local foods. Organic foods were considered "whacky" and expensive. Consumption of local organic food was certainly not a mainstream movement, rather something reserved for people who drove VW buses and wore sandals.

While in Colorado I had a chance to start playing ice hockey again as our resort had a corporate team that played in the town of Breckenridge. I had played hockey most of my life including collegiate hockey. Playing ice hockey at ten thousand feet above sea level was certainly nothing I was used to. I remember the fist time I skated and could not breathe at all; I almost quit on the spot. My teammate and current boss, a short-tempered farm boy from Canada turned corporate spreadsheet jockey, would have no part of that. He was determined to whip me into shape, not only at work, but also at the hockey rink. The hockey team was the perfect outlet to relieve the stress of work. I quickly returned to form and loved the game of hockey again. Those were great times that I miss today.

One morning I woke up and found that my right ring finger was swollen after a game. I thought nothing of it until several days later when it became very inflamed and painful. My doctor diagnosed me with a tumor of the tendon sheath, a rather common finger ailment that would require surgery. These tumors can be cancerous so I was nervous as a schoolboy on a prom date. During surgery the doctor did not find a tumor rather a lot of inflammatory tissue growing all over the tendons of my hand, from the tip of my finger to the wrist. They removed the fatty tissue deposits and sent them to a lab to test; they were not cancerous.

It was non-specific inflammatory tissue that was invading my body. I rehabbed my finger, but about three months later the swelling returned. I then had an MRI which showed the inflammatory tissue was back and now in all my fingers, and my arms. I was referred to a large arthritis clinic in Denver for a full diagnosis. It was determined that I had nonspecific inflammatory arthritis. A serious life change was in my future. After a short few years managing a multi-million dollar budget and many hundreds of seasonal employees in a highly charged, soap opera like atmosphere, I decided to leave the high country and the food business to concentrate on my own wellness and raise our daughter in a better climate. We moved to North Carolina.

In early 2003 we left the high county of Colorado and settled on a twelve-acre horse farm in the scenic rolling hills of western North Carolina. It was country living. I quickly learned to love this special little area of the country; it just felt like home. The smells of cut pasture grass, my John Deere tractor, the allure of the Blue Ridge Mountains right out the door, and the ability to have farm animals all contributed to our new life in the country.

In the first few months we had horses, chickens, dairy goats, and vegetable gardens. We ate homegrown foods to create a healthy and delicious traditional food diet. I found other sources of food nearby including creamy raw milk from Jersey cows, local honey, little farmers' markets, and much more. Never before did I take such an active role in my food purchases; I tried very hard to eat locally and eliminate any foods that were not going to help my recently diagnosed autoimmune condition.

Shortly after the move I began experimenting with different types of foods and food combinations. Things like flax seeds, coconut oil, raw milk, local eggs, dark leafy greens, and vegetables we grew were all part of my discovery. I realized that local and traditional foods were good for my health and the right choice for our children. We were milking goats, collecting eggs, making yogurt, culturing crème frâiche, baking whole wheat bread, eating grass-fed beef, drinking raw cow's milk, juicing fresh vegetables, making pickles, canning tomatoes, drying tomatoes, and many other food-related pursuits. After about six months of immersion in this new way of eating, I knew that this was going to be a lifelong change for us. We were now eating like many Europeans and early Americans, that is to say eating with the seasons. We were growing and sourcing only the best local foods. Another important thing happened during this time: I realized that I missed the food industry. I had studied to receive my health and life insurance license but quickly fell on my face trying to build a business in insurance. I hated the insurance business. I was more focused on diet and our new eating regimen and was truly amazed at how many other parents asked us what we were doing. How did our child actually eat vegetables? How did we make baby food? Where did we find raw milk and eggs? These and many other questions helped spark a passion in me that has led me to my current career in culinary media. Now that others were inquiring about our new skills and wealth of information concerning diet, cooking, and sourcing local foods, I knew I had to share this information with others. I quickly put up a website and the rest as they say is history. Harvest Eating was born!

∽ HARVEST EATING ∽

WHAT IS HARVEST EATING? Harvest Eating is not a fad diet. Rather a lifestyle of cooking and eating using methods that have been practiced for centuries all over the globe. The approach is simple: Buy foods that are fresh and in-season; then prepare them using whole, natural ingredients produced by farmers not chemists. If your second-grader can't read it, you definitely don't want to eat it.

Quite simply, to eat seasonal means to consume fruits and vegetables only during the time of year, or season in which they are harvested. Different seasons bring with them the growth and subsequent harvest of different produce as dictated by the climate in which they are grown. For centuries, many cultures have eaten a diet based solely on fruits and vegetables available only during specific seasons. Over the past fifty years industrialization and the "enhancement" of natural foods has made it possible to eat all fruits and vegetables at any time of the year, regardless of the season.

We Americans do things differently, and that is part of the problems with our diet. Many foods are processed and bought in bulk; therefore, they lack the nutrition they once had. Harvest Eating requires you to become in tuned to what grows in your area, which markets carry local, when the farmer's market is held, and where some "fringe ingredients" can be purchased. The beauty is you can convert a small percentage of your diet and cooking methods using the information contained in this book . . . or go all in. Either way, Harvest Eating can benefit you at any level.

1 | WHAT IS HARVEST EATING?

I. SUSTAINABILITY

LOCAL SEASONAL COOKING

ONE OF THE GREAT TRAGEDIES OF the modern food era is the shift from eating fresh local and seasonal foods to processed foods. I truly believe so much of life is tied to enjoyment, whether from exercise, eating, relationships with family and friends, our work or other pursuits. As humans we have the ability to enjoy many things because we possess highly developed senses and a keen ability to think and feel. Of course I'll speak to the eating part of enjoyment here. As America has changed over the last century, many of the positive aspects of food production and our general eating habits have become a problem. Sure, there have been advancements in farming, food production techniques, and the nutritional know-how of our scientists, but have those advancements borne advantageous fruit? Have they advanced us as a people? Have they translated into any real enjoyment? I would regretfully say no. What I see is a lot of backward movement. The foods we consume are less nutritious. Because we've been convinced we do not have time to cook fresh foods, we buy and eat processed foods. The food industry has learned how to make and skillfully market thousands of new processed food products. They have convinced us it's okay to stock our pantries with manmade foods that have no character and surely have no ability to parlay a full belly into an emotional or physical sense of enjoyment. Sadly, our farmers have learned to raise their yields a tremendous amount by focusing on growing foods that are profitable but not always necessary. These issues are very complex and have been covered in depth in other books. That is not my goal here. I simply want to outline the problem and propose how we can lead healthier lives. My goal is for each and every person who reads this book to take back some of the enjoyment—where our diet is concerned—that has been slowly torn away from our lives. I want you to experience the pleasure that comes from a meal that you had a part in growing, shopping for, and preparing. The more times you experience that enjoyment, the better off we all are collectively as a society.

SLOW FOOD OR NOT

Fortunately in America and beyond there is a resistance, a movement, a growing trend of returning to local, seasonal cooking and the enjoyment good food and drink can bring to our lives. I am excited to be a part of that trend. A few years back, I was a co-founder and establishing board member for the Greenville South Carolina Slow Foods Convivium. Now don't be too concerned about the word *convivium*, I had never heard of it either. The word has its roots in the word *convivial* and the loose translation is: "relating to, occupied with, or fond of feasting, drinking, and good company." Let's rename it *organization*.

The Slow Food organization has become very popular in recent years. Begun by Carlo Petrini of Italy, this burgeoning international organization is a grassroots effort to bring the pleasures of the table back into our lives. Slow Food seeks to protect old recipes, old food ways, and the environment by raising public awareness and teaching us to care for the land, support educational outreach, and protect threatened species of food, whether a plant or animal. It works to advocate for our farmers' well-being and celebrate our food diversity and the pleasures its consumption can bring. Slow Food is the opposite of fast food and all of its perceived and actual negativity.

When I first learned about Slow Food I could not believe there was an organization promoting the very thing I was. As I jumped in I found many people who were just as passionate about local food and seasonality as I was. I knew I needed to be a part of it. I suggest you check it out too: www.slowfood.org.

IMPORTANCE OF GETTING INVOLVED

One of the most important aspects of Harvest Eating is becoming involved with the sourcing of your food. The best chefs are the best shoppers. You won't find a great chef or home cook who is not deeply involved with the purchasing of his or her raw ingredients. It's simply impossible. Seasonal cooking with local foods is not a

new trend. It's been practiced by our great American chefs for many years but has received little attention until recently. Only in the last six to ten years have menus begun listing the sources of certain local foods. When I started Harvest Eating, people did not really care where their pork or vegetables came from. I knew chefs like me were on to something and I knew my message had to be focused on local and seasonal foods to be effective. Gladly, that is my preferred style of cooking, so the fit was natural.

Nothing has taught me more about being connected to the land than getting to know the people who grow my food. As a chef, finding great ingredients is not only fun but necessary to producing great meals. In my local area there are many great sources, and I have learned a lot about local seasonality and foods by building relationships with farmers and growers of all types. I buy local beef, dairy, eggs, vegetables, grains, game, wine and many more staples. Through these purchases, I've learned when and where these items grow near me. I know that the best strawberries come into season in late May and that I'd better eat and cook with them daily because, in sixty days or so they will be gone. I know when the best peaches are in season, as well as corn, bell peppers, tomatoes, collard greens and more. Learning the seasonal growing patterns in your area is key to living the Harvest Eating lifestyle.

LOCAL = SEASONAL

The words *local* and *seasonal* are the very foundation of Harvest Eating. If you eat with the seasons, you will be eating local foods. If you eat local foods you will be eating seasonal foods. There is no way around it. This is true only if you embrace the last chapter of this book. If you are not involved with the regular sourcing of your foods, you can easily be duped into thinking that strawberries in a late August North Carolina market are local. Nope! Those were trucked in from California or some other far-flung place. I am sure some of you reading this will be thinking that you love strawberries so why does it matter where they come from? This line of reasoning just means you're not quite ready for total immersion into Harvest Eating. That's okay. My goal is to help you learn and take small steps that matter. Harvest Eating is flexible, but it also requires some education and the discipline to avoid products that really don't fit the lifestyle. I will gladly admit that when I want blueberries in February I buy frozen organic blueberries—but, only after the bags of fresh local berries I froze last July are gone!

Basically, to eat seasonally is to eat foods when they are available, in the season in which they are harvested. For centuries, we have eaten fresh, locally grown fruits and vegetables. Ever since we began mass producing our foods our mindset has gotten away from supporting the local farmer and gravitated towards saving money. The result is a diet of genetically or chemically modified foods that are often eaten months after they are picked from the ground, and therefore contain only a fraction of their original nutritional value. Eating seasonally has several benefits, it allows you to enjoy the ripest, freshest ingredients possible, it provides an opportunity to support local farmers who transport their goods the shortest distance to your plate, and it also provides an opportunity to experiment with delicious foods you might not have otherwise considered.

With more and more people becoming concerned both about the foods they eat and the environment, organic foods have quickly moved from the fringe to mainstream. Organic foods are foods grown without the assistance of synthetic pesticides, herbicides and fungicides - all chemicals that are potentially harmful to those who consume them, and to the environment.

Organic agriculture methods are focused on promoting and enhancing soil biodiversity, meaning they focus on putting back into the soil the same good things they take from it. That way the soil is able to naturally improve year over year. In 2001 the United States Department of Agriculture and the National Organic Standards Board developed the National Organic Standards. From these standards came the requirement that all products labeled "100% Organic" contain only organically produced ingredients and that any product labeled "Organic" contain at least 95 percent organically grown ingredients.

The term "Certified Organic" is now commonly

found on many products you see today. That mark denotes the product has been certified by an agency accredited by the United States Department of Agriculture and that it meets all the organic standards associated with the production and handling of that product.

Did you know the average meal travels 1500 miles to get to your dinner plate? Eating locally means eating foods that are grown or raised within a relatively short distance from your home. Eating locally will ensure you are consuming the freshest ingredients containing optimal nutritional values.

By eating locally you also help protect the environment by not consuming foods that take large amounts of fuel and energy to ship across the country. As well, you support local farmers and food providers focused on sustainable farming practices while also supporting the contributions they make to your local economy. Eating locally is not always feasible and not always the most convenient thing to do. But, if you can find local food providers in your area and acquire foods from them, you'll find yourself shopping in places with more character than your local store and you'll be doing a world of good for yourself, your local economy and the environment.

CIRCLES OF LIFE

One of the other great learn- ing experiences Harvest Eating can teach is what I call the "circles of life." To me, this is the appreciation of the time, effort, and amazing rewards growing foods can provide. Planting seeds, tending to them, watching them develop into an ingredient we can ultimately eat and, more importantly, derive nutrition from, is an awesome experience. This is why I suggest everybody grow something. Nothing can illustrate the importance of local seasonal foods more than the experience of having eaten something you have grown. A delicious ripe tomato and a few fresh basil leaves from your own garden or window sill is very gratifying to enjoy.

After the move to our twelve-acre farm, starting a garden was one of the very first things we did. Of course we have the land, so planting a one-acre garden was possible. I will be the first to admit that I am a rookie gardener at best. I also admit that I get better yields from a small, raised-bed garden then from our huge one-acre row garden. Nevertheless, gardening has remained a constant, year-round pursuit on our farm. Another "circle of life" experience we have learned about is demonstrated by raising animals. We've had chickens that we kept for eggs and dairy goats we kept for milk. Trust me, there is something special about eating omelets with eggs from your own chickens while drinking a rich, ice-cold glass of last night's goat's milk. Really special! Many of Harvest Eating's followers are avid gardeners and proponents of animal husbandry. By keeping animals you'll quickly learn that when your Saanen dairy goats get into the honeysuckle, their milk will be negatively affected. Also, if you don't handle the milk properly by straining and chilling it, the flavor will be off. If your chickens eat cheap commercial feed, their eggs yolks will be pale and un-appetizing. Conversely, let the hens range free and eat bugs, grasses, and other natural staples of their diet and you'll be rewarded with glowing orange yolks that are incredibly delicious. When your dairy goat eats rich alfalfa hay, good forage and grasses, the milk is sweet and delicious. Learning about the "circles of life" teaches you lessons in quality. Great foods come from sources that are grown or raised the way nature intended. This is why most commercial dairy and beef is not "Harvest Eating Approved."

These simple lessons will give you the confidence to know that how something was raised or grown is very important to the final product's quality. You'll understand that cows fed sugary grain are not going to produce healthy milk. Once you embrace the "circles of life" and look for these processes in their perfect form, you will be eating a cleaner, healthier, and more sustainable diet. You'll be Harvest Eating.

∾ BENEFITS OF LOCAL FOODS ∾

OF COURSE BEYOND THE ABILITY of local foods to please your stomach and mind is a world of benefits they provide to society. I will sheepishly admit these side benefits were not foremost in my mind when I started Harvest Eating. I just wanted the best possible foods for my family and I instinctively knew those were local foods. So what are these societal benefits?

LOCAL ECONOMY
When I buy strawberries down the road from the Cooley family, those funds stay in my local economy. This helps the farmer's family thrive and supports their employees and their ability to maintain their acres as a working farm. I benefit by getting the most delicious strawberries every spring as well as the enjoyment of the fresh air and scenic drive on the visit to their farm. As a side note, Cooley Farms in Chesnee, South Carolina, was one of the first places I took my youngest daughter, Olivia, in the spring to teach her about Harvest Eating.

FARMLAND PRESERVATION
This is huge. Buying local foods—grass-fed beef, raw milk or vegetables—helps maintain farmland. Making a living in farming is getting tougher and tougher for our farmers due to economic pressures and rising input costs. Fuel, fertilizer, hay, electricity, and other inputs of farming are becoming increasingly expensive. In many areas of this country, farms are being lost to development on a daily basis. I have seen this first-hand in my community. A local cattle farmer who had

more than 125 beautiful rolling acres was being slowly surrounded by development. With no way to keep up with rising input costs and make a living, the farmer was forced to sell his land to developers. Within one year their scenic farm had become a strip mall. Another local dairy farmer with 250 acres recently sold his herd because he could not meet expenses that were rising while milk prices were not. At some point, that farm will be a neighborhood. This is a very sad fact, yet one that can be prevented.

On the flip side, I personally know many local farmers who are able to maintain their land because people who follow the Harvest Eating principles eat their products. Some examples include a grass-fed beef operation near me where a nice young family can barely keep up with the strong demand for their beef. Also, a local pasture-based dairy farmer who sells about 20 percent of his milk raw to passionate raw milk drinkers is thriving. These sustainable farms produce great products and consequently have very loyal customers whose patronage helps to ensure their land remains farmland. This is so very important because we do not need more condo developments. We need our farmers to be able to make a living while nurturing the precious land and keeping us supplied with amazing foods. This is why I am so excited about the success of Harvest Eating. It is constantly drawing more people who are willing to support our farmers while helping to make sustainable farming and farmland preservation possible.

PRESERVING TRADITIONAL FARMING VALUES

Coming from a family who farmed was an important factor in why I now make my living promoting the traditional values of farm life. I live on a farm, albeit a small one, but I practice and live these values as a model for my children. Working with the land helps foster a respect for life and work that I feel is very important in this day and age as our lives change with modern times.

Like the appreciation we feel for the EMTs, first responders and firemen who are the unsung heroes rescuing lives as part of their jobs, I have a similar fondness for our farmers. They too are unsung heroes who work long hours doing backbreaking work to provide us with food, to sustain lives. Our farmers are neighbors, friends, and fellow citizens. They do not get into it for the money; they do it because they love the land, the farming lifestyle, and the peace that working in harmony with nature provides. This is why helping to preserve traditional farming values goes hand-in-hand with the purchase of local foods. Every time you or I visit a farm or a farmers' market, or purchase a local food product we are keeping alive the very fabric of our country. Without farms and farmers what would life be like in America? I don't want to know.

RE-ESTABLISHING OUR CONNECTION TO THE LAND

When you finish this book, if you put to use only a few of the principles I describe, you will be re-establishing your own connection to the land. Now I know this may sound a bit eccentric, and I will freely admit that I am no activist, but I do feel strongly about this. The only way to describe this is to tell a story. Every other Wednesday we drive about thirty miles one-way to meet a gentleman named LD Peeler. Mr. Peeler owns and operates a third generation local dairy farm occupied by nice brown Jersey cows. His milk is creamy and delicious. In a word—*incredible*! When I meet him, there are about twenty to fifty other families who also show up at the milk drop to pick up their supply of milk. The same people are always there and have been for years. When I see LD in his blue jean overalls, I inquire about the health of the cows, the price of hay, the recent value of a hundred weight (the price the dairy co-op pays a dairyman for one hundred pounds of milk), recent rainfall (or lack thereof) and other issues that are important to him and to his operation. While it may sound like small talk, every one of these issues is directly correlated to my milk and therefore my connection to the land. Re-establishing a connection to the land and the people who tend to it, whether that means talking with your dairy farmer or visiting your egg-lady, will keep you grounded in the fact that the land and its health are paramount to our survival and to our eating pleasure. In France, winemakers refer to "terroir" meaning the qualities, the climate and the overall effects the land has on wine. Understanding this principle is a good illustration for being connected to the land. My belief is that when someone can re-establish their own connection to the land, their desire to eat farm-fresh foods will become magnified. They will begin understanding that the land around them is part of them. The foods grown locally become an integral part of their lives. When this happens, people's habits change and Harvest Eating becomes part of life.

QUALITY OF LOCAL FOOD

The quality of local food is often higher than that of store-bought foods that have been imported or trucked in from afar. Instinctively, we all sniff, squeeze and fondle foods to see how fresh they are. When you buy local, you are buying freshly harvested foods that are healthier and of higher quality. Foods that are recently harvested have more available nutrition than foods that are picked and stored and shipped. The moment a zucchini is picked the decomposition begins. With each minute that goes by, that zucchini is worse than it was the minute before. You cannot escape this fact. This is why when you buy local freshly-harvested foods, organic or not, you are getting better quality food. Don't be fooled by those lifeless clones in the supermarket which are out of season but somehow look edible. There is always something funky about them, whether it's from a trip around the world or exposure to gases or cold storage. Avoid imported food when possible. Of course, when I want real cheese, this often means buying some that is imported or, at the very least, trucked in. However, the items that are available locally always take precedence in my purchasing habits.

2. SOURCING

IN MID 2003 WHEN MY WIFE AND I started pursuing local foods we were shocked to find so many sources so close to us. The first things we found were eggs. We had been looking for free-range eggs and we asked a clerk at our local health food store if they knew anybody. They pointed us to the bulletin board which was loaded with all types of information. There were local eggs, local beef, CSAs (community sustainable agriculture), and plenty of tail-gate markets listed on their info board. I found a local lady who lived on a beautiful horse farm who raised chickens and sold the eggs to friends and neighbors. I called her to see if she could spare a couple dozen, she obliged and we were hooked. Her chickens had the run of the farm (and barn) and she fed them with high-quality seeds, grains and vegetable scraps. The yolks her chickens produced looked nothing like the eggs you get at the local supermarket. They reminded me of the eggs in Germany and in France which are a deep orange color. One morning while vacationing in Bavaria I made eggs for the relatives we stayed with. I'll never forget the color of the egg yolks, and I remember adding about a quarter cup of rich heavy cream and freshly snipped chives to the eggs. With that much cream, most eggs would wind up pale white, but not these, they were a pumpkin orange color even though I doused them with cream. Needless to say, great eggs have been on our table ever since we found our first source.

In early 2004, when the egg lady ran short because of problems with coyotes, we decided to get our own laying hens because once you have real eggs there is no going back to tasteless, factory-farm eggs. We found a gal who was moving to Taiwan and looking for a home for her twelve laying hens. We gladly gave them a home. Our new hens laid about ten eggs a day. We ate plenty of eggs and gave plenty away too. At the time we were living in our barn apartment, so the hen house was a stones throw away. This was a major problem because as soon as the chickens heard us, twelve maniacal hens would race over and follow our every move, leaving a trail of chicken poop behind them. We ended up giving them to the egg lady in exchange for eggs.

Another fabulous experience we had was learning about real dairy, that is to say dairy products made from cows or goats that graze green pasture. Now the fact that we prefer dairy from cows on pasture might sound strange to you because most people think all cows graze on grass. Unfortunately this is not the case. Just like factory farms that produce pork and beef, there are factory farms that produce milk and other dairy products. These farms, if you can call them that, pack the cows together to get a higher yield. Sometimes they never, *never* let the cows on grass at all. They feed them a diet high in sugary grains, which tends to cause health problems. To prevent sickness and to keep production high, many farms add growth hormones and antibiotics. Abusing the cows like this results in poor health, a sub-standard existence for the cows, and poor quality milk in our glasses.

My research on this subject led us to the point of getting a dairy animal. I remember enjoying the milk right from the tanks in my uncle's barn on his dairy farm and never forgot how fabulously rich and creamy it was. We decided to get a Jersey cow but a visit to a local goat dairy changed our minds. So in 2004 we purchased a very nice Saanen dairy goat with a baby doe by her side. Rose was giving me a gallon of delicious creamy goats milk while her daughter Clarice (named after Rudolph the red nosed reindeer's girlfriend) bounded around the barn always entertaining us. Now before you say, "Goat's milk, yuk. That's gross." Let me illuminate you. Goat's milk from the supermarket is terrible. It is musky, goaty, and just plain bad. However, milk from a goat which is eating a good diet and is harvested with a lot of attention to detail is amazingly delicious. Even my wife who would not get anywhere near a store bought glass of goat's milk loved it! Our doe was elegant, intelligent, fun to be around, and provided a constant supply of milk.

During those first few years we also quickly learned that while we could buy certain locally-grown ingredients like fresh herbs and lettuces at tail-gate markets, growing them at home is easy and much more cost effective. We manage two separate gardens: a warm garden for herbs and a cool garden for lettuces. Our cool garden faces due south, which makes growing in late fall and early spring easy. By doing this, here in the south you can manage to have fresh lettuces about eight months out of the year and certain herbs year round. The hearty herbs with "woody" stems, such as thyme, rosemary, and oregano, will grow year-round in the southern states if the garden is facing south. The tender herbs, such as cilantro, basil, parsley, dill, and chervil , need warmer weather, and so are planted in late April after the last frost to maintain a harvest until the first frost. If you don't have a lot of land, herbs and lettuces, which are expensive to buy, can be grown in small containers or in a sunny window sill.

One of the great things about being on the hunt for local food is the people you meet and the places you get to visit. Local farms and local markets are much more enjoyable to visit then a big-box grocery store. I always took Olivia, my oldest daughter, with me on trips to get food. She visited grass-fed beef ranches, small Jersey dairy farms where we bought milk right from the farmer, local u-pick strawberry farms, blueberry and blackberry farms, and attended Saturday morning farmer's markets with me during warmer months. These continue to be great family outings and we always try to find new places to visit. It's the perfect immersion tool for kids to learn about where their food comes from. They will be much more excited about eating the foods they get from the farmer or even pick themselves.

Sourcing foods is rather easy these days and takes only minimal research to find great places. There has been an explosion of local food guides such as the Edible line of magazines (ediblecommunities.com) which are printed in many cities. These small papers list many local food sources and events that can help get you plugged into the Harvest Eating lifestyle rather quickly in your local area.

Of course if you are going to eat with the seasons you'll need access to local foods. This has become much easier in the last two years with the popularity of local and seasonal cooking. The media has shed much light on this movement. With my efforts on Harvest Eating.com, I hope that I have been an integral part of it as well.

In most parts of the country, people are finding that access to local food is becoming easier. This is a great sign. Another ongoing development is that the number of farmers' markets have nearly doubled since 1994, making a visit to one much more convenient. Also, most communities, both big and small, are setting up tailgate markets and other less formal roadside stands. Many local governments are also involved with providing venues and funding for ambitious locals who want to establish markets.

Another exciting way for people to secure a regular supply of locally-grown, seasonal food is through Community Sustainable Agriculture or CSAs, a movement which is also really taking hold in this country. The premise is quite simple. You buy a share in a farmer's crop yield. Usually it's a monthly fee or sometimes one payment before planting. Then, each week throughout the growing season you are supplied with an equal share of the harvest. Your weekly basket will change as the seasons change and this variety helps to keep recipes changing and foods fresh and delicious. The CSA movement is one reason Harvest Eating was established. Many people new to cooking would join a CSA then use the Internet to find Harvest Eating and ask what they could do with certain produce items they had not cooked or eaten before. This is the reason we provide recipe searches by ingredient category and by season on our website.

Just about everyone should be able to find some locally-grown foods in their immediate area. To make life easy, the Internet is able to assist those in search of local foods. Here are some great web resources that you can use to find information on sustainable foods and databases to find providers.

Local Harvest (www.localharvest.com)
This website has a zip code driven database of thousands of small farms, farm stands and markets all across the country. It's easy to use and very popular.

Sustainable Table (www.sustainabletable.com)

This site has loads of written information, tools for finding foods, handouts, and many other programs that all focus on sustainable food choices. They also have some really cool animated movies called "The Meatrix".

Eat Wild (www.eatwild.com)

Eat Wild is a website that focuses on driving people toward grass fed meats of all types. The site contains many articles by a popular writer named Jo Robinson.

Food Routes (www.foodroutes.org)

Food Routes is a great site that also offers ways to find food and contains in-depth information about the distance food travels from farm to plate.

USDA (apps.ams.usda.gov/FarmersMarkets/)

This handy zip code tool will help you find even the smallest farm markets. This list has greatly expanded in the last few years.

CSAs (www.wilson.edu/csasearch/search.asp)

This college website has a search tool to find CSA's near you.

GROWING FOOD AT HOME

I WOULD BE REMISS IF I DID NOT encourage you to garden at home. Now I am not saying you need a green thumb and acres of land to do it. Growing food at home can be as simple as a few pots of cherry tomatoes and basil, set out in the sun on your back porch or deck. This type of container gardening has become very trendy and it costs very little to get started. On the other hand, getting further involved in gardening is also something I hardily advise.

The act of growing food and the time spent outside doing it is very good for your soul. Most people who advance from container gardening usually make the jump to raised bed gardening. I am a big fan of this method.

Raised bed gardens have several key advantages over traditional row gardening. First off, they are raised, which makes them easier to work in because not as much bending is required. This saves your back from potential aches. Another advantage is they tend to drain better, which is a plus for areas with poor drainage such as the South with its hard clay soil. Proper drainage is key to successful gardening. The other thing I like about raised beds is the soil is less compacted, which eliminates the need for rototilling machinery.

I will admit that old timers seem to prefer traditional row gardening and it remains very popular with local farmers in my region. There certainly is something nostalgic about a neat row garden bustling with seasonal produce, maybe one day I will have the time to tend to my own row garden. For now I am using raised beds and containers.

When we first purchased our farm in 2003 we set out to have a big row garden. I was excited! I bought about thirty different types of seeds so I could grow about every kind of vegetable available. We laid out a row garden, amended the soil, tilled it, planted it, tended to it, then went to Europe for three weeks in July…big mistake. We returned to a mess of weeds and overgrowth. It was very frustrating. We did manage to get a good harvest of herbs, tomatoes and potatoes but most other crops yielded mediocre results at best. That was a good lesson and we scaled back the row garden next year and had better results with less effort.

Finally in year three we switched to raised bed gardens and seemed to find our niche. We typically grow: tomatoes, kale, collard greens, spinach, broccoli, cherry and beefsteak tomatoes, zucchini, basil, thyme, rosemary, oregano, dill, and chives. This year I hope to have a few rows of potatoes as well.

My best advice for beginning gardeners is to start slowly so you do not attempt to many different plants and get overwhelmed. Choose a few key items that can be grown in containers; then see how it goes. I suggest a pot of lettuce, (I like a mix of romaine and some tender greens such as oak leaf, arugula and frissee), also a large pot container with sweet 100 cherry tomatoes and some basic herbs such as basil, thyme, parsley, and rosemary. All this can be purchased for under fifty dollars at most nurseries or home stores.

For those of you who have an eye toward landscape design there are other possibilities to explore. Most home stores sell large half barrels constructed of wood with black iron rings. These are big enough to grow all the herbs you need in one barrel. The same is true for lettuces and tomatoes. These can be strategically placed around your home in sunny areas to not only produce food but to improve curb appeal and create rustic beauty in and around sitting areas.

These barrels also make perfect planters for flowers that are simply beautiful to look at when filled with brightly colored vibrant flowers. I suggest plants like Marigolds and Pansies which do well in containers.

The benefits of growing your own foods are not all summed up in "what can I put on my plate." The experience is more. It's being able to enjoy the outdoors, to hear the birds chirping, seeing the morning sun reflecting on the dew, and smelling the flowering plants in the garden. It's also a great reward to be able to share a basket of everything you grow with friends and neighbors. It's a way to build community.

The nutritional reward for growing your own food is great. The nutrients lost in travel from the farms to your local super stores are substantial. When you pick an ear of corn fresh from the stalk, few people know it's at its highest level of sweetness. As time goes by starches develop and then you have the "Fresh Corn" you find at Walmart. Corn, like other vegetables not only loses nutritional value but actually change its structure as it deteriorates. Growing your own vegetables on the other hand will give you more flavor than you've ever known before. The different varieties you can plant in your garden are endless and will never be found in the local market. Most heirloom varieties cannot survive the long trek from the farm to your grocer. So when you grow heirloom varieties, you have the ability to see into the past, to see what our ancestors planted, shared with one another and passed on to us through their seeds.

While the initial cost of gardening may be a few dollars or a few hundred dollars, depending on the size, as the years go by is far less for each vegetable.

Now that we've established some of the benefits of gardening we can look deeper into some useful tips on getting the best out of your labor of love. I mentioned my affinity for raised bed gardens and I'd like to expound. They are easy to care for. The size of a raised bed should be large enough for you to be able to reach to the middle with ease from any point. This makes weeding a breeze. This also gives you an opportunity to "companion plant" to grow different vegetables and herbs that are beneficial to each other. Like tomatoes and basil love to grow together because of the natural insect repellent found in the basil and the fact that basil attracts bees that pollinate the tomatoes. Raised beds can also offer the ability to reap one area and sow another simultaneously. Water management is a very important benefit. Some plants like a lot of water while others not as much. With raised beds this couldn't be an easer problem to solve… So off you go, start a raised bed today!

Now that you have started your garden and are ready to use some of the delicious foods, there are some helpful tips you will want to know. For instance, when picking flowering herbs, such as lavender, pick them in the morning before the flower opens completely and after the moisture has evaporated. This will protect it from rot. As for leaves and stem herbs pick these just before the plant begins to flower. This is when the essential oils are at their strongest.

Here are a few sources for gardening know-how and supplies that I recommend.

SEEDS

Johnny's Seeds (www.johnnyseeds.com) my personal favorite.

Burpee (www.burpee.com)

Park Seed (www.parkseed.com)

Other Gardening Supplies

Gardeners Supply (www.gardeners.com)

Smith & Hawkin (www.smithandhawkin.com)

ONLINE RESOURCES

About.com (gardening.about.com)

Garden Guides (www.gardenguides.com)

National Gardening Association (www.garden.org)

∾ HOW TO USE THIS BOOK ∾

E ACH RECIPE IN THIS BOOK IS marked with a seasonal symbol to indicate when the main ingredients are most fresh. These symbols are to be used as a general guide. Depending on where you live, some foods are available earlier or later in the year. Some recipes are marked with multiple symbols to indicate that the ingredients are fresh in various seasons. There are a few that are good all year. Here are the symbols:

❋ = spring

☀ = summer

🍁 = fall

❄ = winter

2 | RECIPES

3 | BREAKFASTS AND BREADS

PANCAKES ✺ ✲ ✳ ✺

PREP TIME: 5 MINUTES | COOK TIME: 10 MINUTES | READY IN: 15 MINUTES

Use the Harvest Eating pancake mix recipe to make wonderful thin pancakes. I like to use plenty of butter to create that nice brown color on the pancakes. With some dark coffee and real Vermont grade A amber pure maple syrup, what could be better?

MAKES 10 SERVINGS

1 cup Harvest Eating pancake mix (page 268)

1 cup organic milk

1 tablespoon ground flax seeds

1 tablespoon wheat germ

1 free-range egg, beaten

1 tablespoon clarified or regular butter

1. Combine the pancake mix, milk, flax seeds, wheat germ, and egg in a large bowl to make the batter. This can be made up to an hour in advance.

2. Heat a nonstick griddle, nonstick skillet or a properly-seasoned cast-iron skillet over medium heat. Add the butter. Pour about ¼ cup of the pancake batter into the pan and cook.

3. Look for some browning to occur before flipping each pancake.

4. Serve them with your favorite toppings.

Chef's Note: To clarify the butter, heat 25 percent more butter than you'll need in a pan over medium heat until foam appears. Scape off the foam and slowly pour off the butter fat into a separate bowl, being careful not to pour off any of the water in the bottom of the pan.

ZUCCHINI-WALNUT BREAD ☀ ❀

PREP TIME: 15 MINUTES | COOK TIME: 60 MINUTES | READY IN: 75 MINUTES

Making zucchini-walnut bread is a good way to use all your extra zucchini in the summertime. A good tip is to grate lots of zucchini into two-cup measures; then freeze them so you can make zucchini-walnut bread in the future.

MAKES 15 SERVINGS

3 large free-range eggs

2 cups granulated sugar

1 cup pure olive oil

1 teaspoon vanilla extract

1 teaspoon baking powder

1 teaspoon baking soda

¾ teaspoon ground cinnamon

3 cups all-purpose flour

2 cups grated zucchini

1 cup chopped walnuts

1. Preheat the oven to 350°F.

2. Combine the eggs and sugar in a large work bowl. Whisk well to combine, then whisk in the oil and vanilla.

3. Sift the baking powder, baking soda, cinnamon, and flour together in a bowl. Slowly add the dry to the wet ingredients stirring until well combined.

4. Add the zucchini and walnuts and mix well.

5. Add the batter to a greased 8 x 4 x 2-inch loaf pan until it is three-quarters full.

6. Bake for 1 hour or until a toothpick or tester comes out clean. Cool on a rack before slicing.

Chef's Note: Zucchini-walnut bread can be frozen after it's completely cooled.

PARMESAN-CHIVE EGG SOUFFLÉ ✳

PREP TIME: 15 MINUTES | COOK TIME: 45 MINUTES | READY IN: 60 MINUTES

Never fear soufflés; they are easy to make. Using chives and good Parmesan make this lunch dish a pleasure to eat.

MAKES 4 TO 6 SERVINGS

4 large free-range eggs

Kosher salt, to taste

Freshly ground black pepper, to taste

2 tablespoons organic half-and-half

3 tablespoons grated Parmigiano-Reggiano cheese

2 tablespoons minced fresh chives

2 tablespoons organic unsalted butter

1. Preheat the oven to 350°F.

2. Break the eggs into a work bowl. Season them with the salt and pepper. Add the half-and-half and whisk until well combined.

3. Whisk in the Parmigiano-Reggiano and chives.

4. Grease a heavy ovenproof dish or soufflé pan on all sides with the butter.

5. Pour the mixture into the dish and bake for 45 minutes or until the soufflé is brown on top.

Chef's Note: You can substitute fresh thyme or tarragon for the fresh chives.

SPINACH WITH EGGS AND FRESH CHIVES ✳

PREP TIME: 5 MINUTES | COOK TIME: 5 MINUTES | READY IN: 10 MINUTES

A simple little recipe that brings big flavors thanks to the chives and Gruyère cheese, one of my favorite cheeses. Be sure not to overcook the eggs. If they are dry in the pan, they will be dry on the plate.

MAKES 2 SERVINGS

2 tablespoons extra-virgin olive oil

1 cup organic spinach leaves

2 free-range eggs, farm-fresh if possible

2 tablespoons organic cream or whole milk

2 tablespoons Gruyère cheese

Kosher salt, to taste

Freshly ground black pepper, to taste

Chopped fresh chives, for garnish

1. In a nonstick skillet over medium heat, combine the oil and spinach, cook until spinach wilts, about 1 minute.

2. Combine the eggs with the cream or milk in a bowl and beat vigorously. Add the beaten eggs to the skillet with the spinach and cook until they are soft scrambled.

3. Add the cheese and cook until melted. Season with the salt and pepper and serve garnished with chives.

Chef's Note: Serve with sprouted grain toast and real butter.

STEEL-CUT IRISH OATMEAL ✳

PREP TIME: 3 MINUTES | COOK TIME: 30 MINUTES | READY IN: 33 MINUTES

This recipe creates a very healthy homemade oatmeal that blows away instant oats. It is a totally different product. I make big batches of this; then store for up to seven days in the refrigerator. I reheat it in a pot with some milk and serve it as quick oatmeal. This is the breakfast I eat before doing farm chores on winter days.

MAKES 4 SERVINGS

1¾ cups organic milk

1 teaspoon vanilla extract

⅓ cup steel-cut oats

1 tablespoon organic butter

1 teaspoon Vermont maple syrup

2 tablespoons heavy cream

¼ cup dried cherries

1. Heat the milk and vanilla in a saucepan over medium heat. Bring to a simmer.

2. Add the oats and bring back to a simmer. Reduce the heat to medium low and cook for 30 minutes

3. Add the butter, syrup, cream, and cherries. Stir until well mixed.

Cook's Note: Oatmeal is a great canvas for additional healthy ingredients, such as yogurt, walnuts, flax seeds and fruit. Make a big batch, then portion and freeze. If you like the cherries to be plump, add them to the pot of cooking oatmeal about five minutes before finished to absorb some moisture.

4 | SANDWICHES AND APPETIZERS

CHICKEN SALAD-STUFFED AVOCADO ☀

PREP TIME: 15 MINUTES | READY IN: 15 MINUTES

This is a delicious and healthy twist on the classic chicken salad. I use the meat of ripe avocados in the salad; then serve it in the scooped out avocado shell. The crème fraîche instead of store-bought mayonnaise is the secret to this recipe.

MAKES 2 SERVINGS

1 Hass avocado

1 cup diced poached chicken

2 tablespoons minced celery

½ shallot, minced

½ teaspoon Dijon mustard

3 tablespoons crème fraîche

2 tablespoons sliced almonds

Pinch of Harvest Eating House
  Seasoning (page 278)

1. Cut the avocado in half. Remove the pit and discard.

2. Cut a small slice off the back of each half of the avocado shell, so they will sit level and become little "bowls" for the salad. Scoop out each half of the avocado and chop it into small pieces.

3. Combine the avocado, chicken, celery, shallot, mustard, crème fraîche, almonds, and seasoning in a mixing bowl. Fold carefully to incorporate but not mash all of the ingredients.

4. To serve, scoop large portions of the salad into each empty avocado half.

CHICKEN SALAD FINGER SANDWICH ❋✳❋❋

PREP TIME: 10 MINUTES | READY IN: 10 MINUTES

This light chicken salad is wonderful due to the addition of crème frâiche and tarragon, which, in my opinion, is an underused herb. Delicate flavors are really nice on soft wheat bread.

MAKES 5½ CUPS

5 cups cooked, cooled and shredded chicken breast

¼ cup crème fraîche

1 tablespoon fresh tarragon, minced

2 tablespoons minced celery

1 tablespoon minced shallot

Kosher salt, to taste

Freshly ground black pepper, to taste

2 thin whole wheat bread slices

1. Combine the chicken, crème fraîche, tarragon, celery, shallot, salt, and pepper. Stir until well combined.

2. Place approximately ½ cup of the chicken salad on the bread slices, cut in half and serve.

Chef's Note: The tarragon in this chicken salad really makes the difference. If you are looking to cut calories you might consider using plain yogurt instead of crème fraîche.

ORGANIC SALAD WRAP ☀

PREP TIME: 7 MINUTES | READY IN: 7 MINUTES

This is a healthy, low-carb wrap with fresh vegetables and a homemade French Vinaigrette. You can't help but feel extra healthy after eating this light, refreshing and satisfying wrap. Young fresh goat cheese can be substituted for the feta cheese.

MAKES 4 SERVINGS

2 cups organic green leaf lettuce

1 cup organic baby spinach leaves

½ cup shredded cabbage

Kosher salt, to taste

1 to 2 tablespoons French Vinaigrette (page 271)

1 medium carrot

2 (10-inch) whole wheat tortillas

3 tablespoons feta cheese, crumbled

1. Chop leaf lettuce, spinach, and cabbage into small pieces. Place in a mixing bowl. Add salt and French vinaigrette. Toss lightly to coat.

2. Peel and shred the carrot. Add to the mixture. Taste and add more vinaigrette if needed to coat and toss again.

3. Mound the mixture evenly on each tortilla and top with feta. Roll tightly. Cut in half and serve.

VEGAN WRAP ☀

This delicious vegan wrap with homemade Meyer lemon hummus makes a great meal. The avocado provides some girth, and the lettuce is very refreshing. It's the perfect vegan food.

MAKES 2 SERVINGS

½ cup Meyer lemon hummus
   (page 53)

2 medium whole wheat tortilla
   wraps

½ cup chopped lettuce

4 slices avocado

2 tablespoons French Vinaigrette
   (page 271)

1. Spread about ¼ cup of the hummus onto each wrap. Then place the lettuce and avocado in the center of the wrap and dress with the French vinaigrette.

2. Carefully roll up the wrap and cut in half to serve.

ROASTED RED PEPPER HUMMUS WRAP ☀

This roasted red pepper hummus is delicious and interesting. The sweetness that the dates bring to the wrap is unexpected.

MAKES 2 SERVINGS

½ cup red pepper hummus (page 52)

1 whole wheat tortilla wrap

2 dates, pitted and halved

4 avocado slices

1 cup chopped organic lettuce

1 tablespoon Orange Herb Vinaigrette (page 239)

1. Spread the hummus on the tortilla and arrange the dates and avocado slices on top.

2. Toss the lettuce in the vinaigrette and add it to the wrap. Carefully roll up the wrap and cut in half to serve.

QUESADILLA WITH CHICKEN AND PINTO BEANS ❋ ❋ ❋ ❋

PREP TIME: 10 MINUTES | COOK TIME: 15 MINUTES | READY IN: 25 MINUTES

Quesadillas are a great snack food and perfect for lunch. I often serve this one to my family for a quick nutritious lunch.

MAKES 4 SERVINGS

2 (8-inch) flour tortillas

1 cup chopped, poached all-natural chicken

½ cup pinto beans

½ cup shredded sharp cheddar cheese

1 tablespoon fresh cilantro

¼ teaspoon cumin

2 tablespoons salsa, for garnish

1 tablespoon sour cream, for garnish

1. Heat a large frying pan over low heat. Top a tortilla with the chicken, beans, cheese, and cilantro. Sprinkle with cumin and cover with the second tortilla. Cook one tortilla on one side and then flip.

2. Continue cooking until the ingredients are hot and the cheese is melted. Remove from heat and cut into quarters. Garnish with additional cilantro, salsa, and sour cream.

bad recipe

ARTICHOKE GRATIN ✳

This dish is best made in the spring when artichokes are in season and at their freshest. Of course preparing artichokes can be challenging and time consuming for novice cooks with limited knife skills. I give my blessing to use frozen artichokes in water as a substitute for this dish.

MAKES 6 SERVINGS

2 (10-ounce) packages frozen artichoke hearts

1 tablespoon lemon juice

3 tablespoons plain breadcrumbs

1 tablespoon freshly grated Parmesan cheese

1 teaspoon dried Italian seasoning

1 garlic clove, minced

1 teaspoon extra-virgin olive oil

1. Preheat the oven to 375°F.

2. Coat a 9-inch glass pie plate with cooking spray.

3. Place the artichokes in a colander and rinse well with cold water to separate. Drain well, then pat dry with paper towels. Place in the prepared pie plate and sprinkle with the lemon juice.

4. In a small bowl, combine the breadcrumbs, cheese, Italian seasoning, garlic, and oil. Sprinkle the mixture evenly over the artichokes.

5. Bake for 15 minutes, or until the topping is golden.

TOMATO AND AVOCADO SANDWICH ☀

PREP TIME: 5 MINUTES | READY IN: 5 MINUTES

This delicious and healthy tomato and avocado sandwich is great for a summer lunch. The cilantro butter gives it a nice texture and flavor. It's perfect with a glass of Riesling on a hot summer day.

MAKES 1 SERVING

1 tablespoon fresh cilantro, minced

2 tablespoons organic unsalted butter, softened

2 slices good bread

½ cup organic lettuce

3 (¼-inch thick) slices organic ripe tomato

½ avocado, pitted and sliced

Kosher salt, to taste

Freshly ground black pepper, to taste

1. Combine the cilantro with the butter. Mix well and spread on the bread.

2. Top with the lettuce.

3. Add the tomato and avocado slices and season with the salt and pepper. Top with the remaining bread slice.

Chef's Note: I can't stress enough that this tomato and avocado sandwich needs fresh, high-quality tomatoes and a good ripe avocado.

BACON CHEDDAR CHEESEBURGER ☀

I make this burger from lean, grass-fed beef from local farmers. It is amazing. Try it the next time you cook on your grill. You will never go back to grain-fed beef.

MAKES 4 SERVINGS

1 pound grass-fed ground beef

1 teaspoon garlic pepper seasoning

1 teaspoon Worcestershire sauce

1 teaspoon kosher salt

¼ teaspoon freshly ground black pepper

4 buns

1 grilled poblano pepper, sliced

1 grilled red or green bell pepper, sliced

4 slices cheddar cheese

8 slices applewood bacon or your favorite, cooked

1. Preheat a charcoal or gas grill to medium high.

2. Combine the ground beef, garlic pepper seasoning, Worcestershire sauce, salt and pepper and form into patties.

3. Grill until they are done to your taste.

4. Serve on buns with the roasted peppers, cheese, and bacon.

Chef's Note: Add the type of condiments you like, and I suggest toasting the buns. To grill the peppers, place them on the hottest part of the grill, turning them frequently until the skin is blackened.

TOMATO BRUSCHETTA ☀

This simple and delicious appetizer is a breeze to make and is a hit at most parties. It's best when the tomatoes and basil are abundant. In Italy they grill the bread over a wood fire. A toaster oven or grill works too.

MAKES 6 SERVINGS

6 slices of ciabatta bread

2 garlic cloves

3 whole fresh tomatoes

Kosher salt, to taste

A few twists of freshly ground black pepper

1 bunch fresh basil, sliced into thin strips (chiffonade)

½ cup extra-virgin olive oil

½ cup grated Parmigiano-Reggiano cheese

1. Toast or grill the ciabatta bread until lightly browned.

2. Rub each slice of bread with the garlic cloves. The garlic will break down slightly because the bread surface is abrasive.

3. Cut the tomatoes in half and squeeze out as much of the seeds and liquid as possible. Then rub the tomato halves all over the bread to get the tomato meat on the bread.

4. Add the salt, pepper, and the basil chiffonade.

5. Drizzle each piece of bread with the extra-virgin olive oil and add the cheese.

ROASTED RED PEPPER HUMMUS ☀

PREP TIME: 5 MINUTES | READY IN: 5 MINUTES

Hummus is very easy to make, and this one is loaded with bell pepper flavor. Making hummus at home will save you money, and it tastes better, too.

MAKES 8 SERVINGS

- 2 (15-ounce) cans garbanzo beans, rinsed well and drained
- 3 tablespoons tahini paste
- 2 tablespoons freshly squeezed lemon juice
- ¾ cup extra-virgin olive oil
- 1 cup roasted red peppers
- 1 garlic clove, minced
- 1 teaspoon ground cumin
- ⅛ teaspoon cayenne pepper
- 1 teaspoon kosher salt
- ¼ teaspoon freshly ground black pepper

1. Combine the beans, tahini paste, lemon juice, oil, peppers, garlic, cumin, cayenne pepper, salt and pepper in the bowl of your food processor and pulse until the hummus is smooth.

2. Adjust the seasoning with additional salt and pepper to taste. Serve with tortilla chips or toasted bread.

MEYER LEMON ROSEMARY HUMMUS ☀

PREP TIME: 5 MINUTES | COOK TIME: 5 MINUTES | READY IN: 10 MINUTES

Flavorful Meyer lemon, pungent rosemary and flavorings of the Mediterranean make this hummus delicious. I hope you try this because it is very easy and much better than store bought. I eat this hummus often in warm months as a wrap with greens from my garden.

MAKES 6 SERVINGS

⅓ cup extra-virgin olive oil

2 garlic cloves

1 teaspoon fresh rosemary leaves, finely minced

2 (15-ounce) cans organic garbanzo beans, rinsed and drained

Zest from 1 Meyer lemon

½ teaspoon kosher sea salt

¼ teaspoon curry powder

¼ teaspoon smoked paprika

¼ teaspoon cumin powder

Juice of 3 whole Meyer lemons

⅛ teaspoon freshly ground black pepper

¼ cup tahini paste

1. Heat the oil in a small saucepot over low heat.

2. Add the garlic and rosemary and cook for 3 minutes to infuse the oil. Do not brown the garlic.

3. Combine the garbanzo beans, lemon zest, sea salt, curry powder, paprika, cumin, lemon juice, pepper, and tahini paste in the bowl of a food processor. Add the infused oil mixture and process all the ingredients to a smooth paste.

Chef's Note: Enjoy this spread with toasted pita bread or in a wrap with fresh sprouts, shredded cheese and chopped lettuce.

CRABMEAT-STUFFED TOMATOES ☀

PREP TIME: 15 MINUTES | COOK TIME: 25 MINUTES | READY IN: 40 MINUTES

This simple appetizer or side dish uses delicious jumbo lump crabmeat to add a luxurious flavor and texture to seasonal tomatoes. Beefsteak tomatoes are the perfect nesting spot for a mixture of crabmeat, aromatic herbs, and tangy Gruyère cheese.

MAKES 2 SERVINGS

2 large organic beefsteak tomtoes

2 tablespoons sour cream

2 tablespoons real mayonnaise

1 teaspoon chopped fresh tarragon

1 teaspoon chopped fresh thyme

1 teaspoon chopped fresh basil

1 teaspoon chopped fresh parsley or oregano

2 tablespoons grated Parmigiano-Reggiano cheese

¼ teaspoon cayenne pepper

1 (16-ounce) can fresh crabmeat

2 drops hot sauce or Tabasco

Kosher salt, to taste

Freshly ground black pepper, to taste

½ cup shredded Gruyère cheese

¼ cup breadcrumbs

1. Preheat the oven to 350°F.

2. Cut the tomatoes in half, and scoop out some seeds and flesh to allow room for the crab stuffing; do not break the wall of the tomatoes.

3. In a medium bowl, combine the sour cream, mayonnaise, tarragon, thyme, basil, parsley, Parmigiano-Reggiano cheese, cayenne, crabmeat, hot sauce, salt, and pepper. Mix well.

4. Stuff the crabmeat mixture into the tomato halves.

5. Top each tomato half with Gruyère cheese and breadcrumbs and bake for 25 minutes until bubbly and starting to brown.

CHIPOTLE SHRIMP COCKTAIL ☀ ✺

PREP TIME: 15 MINUTES | COOK TIME: 5 MINUTES | READY IN: 20 MINUTES

A tangy twist makes this cocktail sauce quite special. Chipotle peppers add a smoky heat and make this cocktail sauce slightly fiery, slightly smoky, and delicious.

MAKES 4 SERVINGS

SHRIMP

10 large shrimp, peeled and deveined

1 bay leaf

5 black peppercorns

1 tablespoon Old Bay seasoning

4 whole cloves

Juice of 2 medium lemons

4 tablespoons Worcestershire sauce

SAUCE

1 canned chipotle chile pepper

½ organic white onion, diced

1¼ cups crushed tomatoes

3 tablespoons freshly squeezed lime juice

¼ cup chopped fresh cilantro

1 teaspoon kosher salt

A few twists of freshly ground black pepper

3 tablespoons ketchup

1. **For the shrimp:** Bring a large pot of water to boil.

2. Add the bay leaf, peppercorns, Old Bay, whole cloves, lemon juice, and Worcestershire sauce to the boiling water. Allow the seasonings to infuse the water for 1 minute.

3. Add the shrimp, return the water to a boil, and boil the shrimp for 3 minutes. Drain and place the shrimp in an ice bath to stop the cooking process.

4. **For the sauce:** Combine the chipotle pepper, onion, tomatoes, lime juice, cilantro, salt, pepper, and ketchup in a food processor. Blend well to make a sauce. Adjust seasonings to taste.

5. Serve shrimp cold with the sauce.

5 | SOUPS AND SALADS

CREAM OF TOMATO SOUP ☀

PREP TIME: 10 MINUTES | COOK TIME: 10 MINUTES | READY IN: 20 MINUTES

Since this is a perennial favorite, everyone should learn how to make a delicious and easy cream of tomato soup.

MAKES 4 SERVINGS

1 (28-ounce) can organic plum tomatoes

2 tablespoons extra-virgin olive oil

½ cup minced white onion

Kosher salt, to taste

Freshly ground black pepper, to taste

2 tablespoons all-purpose flour

¼ cup organic heavy cream

1 teaspoon chopped fresh chives, for garnish

1. Purée the tomatoes in a blender.

2. Heat the olive oil in a medium saucepan over medium heat. Add the onion and season with salt and pepper. Sauté the onion until it is soft but not brown.

3. Make a roux by adding the flour to the saucepan and cook the flour and onion for 1 to 2 minutes.

4. Add the puréed tomatoes and cream to the pan. Re-season and stir to combine all the ingredients.

5. Cover and bring to a simmer. To serve, garnish with fresh chives.

Chef's Note: Fresh ingredients are best, of course. Replace the canned tomatoes with fresh, skinned Roma tomatoes when available. Serve this soup with a grilled cheese sandwich for a great comfort-food treat.

ARTICHOKE SOUP ✳

PREP TIME: 5 MINUTES | COOK TIME: 25 MINUTES | READY IN: 30 MINUTES

This artichoke soup is easy to make, very satisfying, and nice to serve at dinner parties.

MAKES 6 SERVINGS

1½ tablespoons extra-virgin olive oil

1 medium shallot, diced

2 whole garlic cloves, minced

1 (16-ounce) can artichoke hearts, drained and chopped

4 cups organic chicken stock

½ cup organic heavy cream

Pinch of kosher salt

Pinch of freshly ground black pepper

1. Heat the oil in a heavy pot over medium heat. Add the shallot and garlic and sauté for 2 minutes.

2. Add the artichoke hearts, chicken stock, and cream. Bring the soup to a slow boil.

3. Season with salt and pepper. Purée the soup in batches in a blender until smooth or use an immersion blender.

Chef's Note: This soup can be served chunky too. Either style is great served with crisp bread. A splash of fresh lemon juice makes a nice finishing garnish for the soup.

CREAM OF MUSHROOM SOUP ✻

PREP TIME: 15 MINUTES | COOK TIME: 20 MINUTES | READY IN: 35 MINUTES

This is a deliciously earthy wild mushroom soup made with crimini and shittake mushrooms and fresh thyme. It's a perfect soup for a dinner party menu that features a crispy grilled pizza.

MAKES 4 TO 6 SERVINGS

2 tablespoons extra-virgin olive oil

¼ cup diced white onion

2 garlic cloves, minced

½ cup minced organic celery

Kosher salt, to taste

Freshly ground black pepper, to taste

2 cups mushrooms (shittake and crimini), sliced

¼ cup dry white wine

2 tablespoons chopped fresh thyme leaves

1 quart organic, low-sodium chicken broth

½ cup organic heavy cream

Fresh chives, for garnish

1. Heat the olive oil in a large pot over medium heat. Add the onion, garlic, and celery and sauté for 2 to 3 minutes to release the flavors. Season with salt and pepper.

2. Add the mushrooms to the pan. Adjust the seasoning to taste. Cook for about 10 minutes, or until the mushrooms are nicely caramelized.

3. Carefully pour the white wine into the pan. Use a spatula to scrape up all of the caramelized bits and deglaze the pan. Continue to cook until reduced by about three-quarters.

4. Add the fresh thyme to the mushrooms and mix well. Then add the chicken broth and cream. Adjust the seasonings, if needed.

5. Cover and bring to a simmer.

6. Using an immersion blender or working in batches in a regular blender, purée the soup.

7. To serve, garnish with fresh chives and a drizzle of extra-virgin olive oil.

Chef's Note: Fresh thyme and mushrooms go together very well! This soup, served with a tossed salad and scrambled eggs, makes a delicious lunch.

SPRING ASPARAGUS SOUP ✿

PREP TIME: 10 MINUTES | COOK TIME: 25 MINUTES | READY IN: 35 MINUTES

When asparagus are in season, this soup is always on the menu. I like to use smaller Asparagus when making this dish as I feel they have a better flavor.

MAKES 4 SERVINGS

1 bunch organic asparagus, reserve the tips or top 1½ inches for step 1 and the stems for step 3

1 tablespoon pure olive oil

1 shallot, sliced

1 garlic clove, sliced

Kosher salt, to taste

Freshly ground black pepper, to taste

1 quart chicken broth

½ cup organic half-and-half, optional

Sour cream or crème fraîche, for garnish

2 tablespoons chopped chives, for garnish

1. Steam the asparagus tips for 3 to 4 minutes until just tender, then run under cold water to stop cooking. Set aside.

2. Heat the olive oil in heavy pot over medium heat. Sweat the shallots and garlic for 1 minute. Season with salt and pepper.

3. Add the chicken broth and asparagus stems; simmer for 15 to 20 minutes until tender.

4. Purée the broth and asparagus stems in the pot with an immersion blender, or in batches using a regular blender or food processor, until smooth and creamy. Strain the puréed soup with a fine mesh strainer forcing as much liquid through as possible.

5. Add the half-and-half, if using, and adjust the seasonings to taste.

6. Garnish with the reserved, cooked asparagus spears and sour cream or crème fraîche. Top with fresh thyme leaves.

Cooks Note: Use a cornstarch slurry (2 tablespoons cornstarch, 1 tablespoon cold water to form a paste) to thicken the simmering soup.

FRENCH ONION SOUP ✻ ✦

PREP TIME: 5 MINUTES | COOK TIME: 70 MINUTES | READY IN: 75 MINUTES

This simple soup is rich tasting and has a fantastic onion flavor with great texture and sweetness. It is finished with an artisan bread crouton topped with melted Gruyère cheese.

MAKES 4 SERVINGS

3 tablespoons pure olive oil

2 large sweet onions, thinly sliced

3 tablespoons sherry wine

2 pints beef broth

Kosher salt, to taste

A few twists of freshly ground black pepper

4 slices good-quality artisan bread

¾ cup grated Gruyère cheese

Fresh thyme leaves, for garnish

1. Heat the oil in a heavy-bottomed pot over medium heat. Add the sliced onions and cook for 2 minutes, stirring constantly. Reduce the heat to low. Cover and cook the onions for 30 minutes.

2. Remove the lid and continue cooking the onions until they become a deep, rich mahogany color, about 15 minutes. Add the sherry wine and deglaze the pan.

3. Add the beef broth and cook for another 20 minutes, still over low heat. Season with salt and pepper. Preheat the broiler to high.

4. Divide the soup among four ovenproof serving bowls.

5. Top each with a slice of bread and some of the grated Gruyère cheese. Place under the broiler for 5 minutes or until the cheese is slightly browned. To serve, garnish with a few thyme leaves.

CORN CHOWDER ❋

Here is a delicious, seasonal chowder with fresh, roasted summer sweet corn. I also use up some extra zucchini is this soup, too. The chipotle pepper is optional, but I think it belongs.

MAKES 8 SERVINGS

2 tablespoons pure olive oil

¼ cup diced white onion

2 garlic cloves, chopped

Kosher salt, to taste

Freshly ground black pepper, to taste

1 whole chipotle pepper, chopped

¼ cup chopped local tomato

½ cup chopped zucchini

2 cups roasted sweet corn, removed from ears

1 quart Chicken Stock (page 278)

1 cup organic heavy cream

2 tablespoons fresh cilantro

1. Heat a heavy Dutch oven over medium heat. Add the oil, onion and garlic. Season with the salt and pepper and sauté for 2 minutes.

2. Add the minced chipotle pepper, tomato, and zucchini and continue cooking for another minute or two. Add the roasted corn kernels, stock and cream.

3. Bring the mixture to a boil over high heat, then reduce heat to low, cover and cook for about 20 minutes.

4. Purée the soup to the desired consistency using an immersion blender, standard blender or food processor. Garnish with fresh cilantro.

Chef's Note: The soup can be forced through a fine sieve such as a chinois to produce a very smooth texture, however I prefer a chunkier style. In fact, you don't even need to purée it at all.

ZUCCHINI AND TOMATO STEW ☀

PREP TIME: 10 MINUTES | COOK TIME: 25 MINUTES | READY IN: 35 MINUTES

This is a delicious and easy recipe, and a great way to use your summer zucchini and tomatoes. They are sautéed into a delicious stew with fresh basil and Parmigiano-Reggiano cheese.

MAKES 10 SERVINGS

2 tablespoons extra-virgin olive oil

½ cup minced organic white onion

2 garlic cloves, minced

2 cups diced local zucchini

1 cup diced local tomato

Kosher salt, to taste

Freshly ground black pepper, to taste

2 tablespoons minced fresh basil

2 tablespoons grated Parmigiano-Reggiano cheese

1. Heat a stainless steel skillet over medium heat. Add the oil, onion, and garlic and sauté for 1 minute.

2. Add zucchini and tomato and continue cooking for 20 to 25 minutes.

3. Season with salt and pepper.

4. Toward the end of the cooking time, add the basil. At the end of the cooking time, add the cheese.

Chef's Note: This dish is best made with fresh zucchini and tomatoes that are in season where you live and at their best. The final consistency should be soft, not mushy so adjust cooking time accordingly. This can be used as a stuffing in a chicken breast, in tacos, over rice, etc.

TORTILLA SOUP ☀

PREP TIME: 10 MINUTES | COOK TIME: 25 MINUTES | READY IN: 35 MINUTES

This soup is really intense in both flavor and certainly in texture. When served, people usually start off by saying, "WOW!" The next thing they say is "can I have another bowl?" Chipotle chile peppers are smoked jalapeños; pasilla chiles are blackish-brown in color. Both are sold in most grocery stores.

MAKES 6 SERVINGS

3 tablespoons pure or light olive oil

½ cup minced onion

1 garlic clove, minced

1 tablespoon tomato paste

1 chipotle chile, minced

2 whole dried pasilla chiles, seeds removed and cut into strips and soaked for 10 minutes

4 cups organic chicken broth

Kosher salt, to taste

Freshly ground black pepper, to taste

1½ cups tortilla strips or chips

Crema

¼ cup diced avocado

4 tablespoons minced fresh cilantro

1. Add the oil, onion and garlic to a saucepot or deep skillet. Sauté or "sweat" them over low heat for 2 minutes.

2. Add the tomato paste and stir and cook for 5 minutes.

3. Add the chipotle and pasilla chiles.

4. Add the chicken broth. Stir well and season with the salt and pepper.

5. Bring the mixture to a simmer and cook for 5 minutes.

6. Place the tortilla strips in a serving bowl. Add the soup. Top with the crema, avocado and fresh cilantro.

Chef's Note: Crema can be made by thinning sour cream with a few tablespoons of half-and-half. Other dried chilies can be substituted for the pasilla.

PORTUGUESE KALE AND POTATO SOUP ❧

PREP TIME: 10 MINUTES | COOK TIME: 45 MINUTES | READY IN: 55 MINUTES

Kale and potatoes cooked together in rich chicken broth become a fantastic comfort food feast. The chorizo brings loads of flavor with its pungent dose of paprika and garlic.

MAKES 10 SERVINGS

3 tablespoons extra-virgin olive oil

3 garlic cloves, minced

Kosher salt, to taste

Freshly ground black pepper, to taste

½ cup sliced onions

1 quart chicken broth

3 russet potatoes, peeled and diced

6 ounces chorizo, cooked

5 cups fresh kale, chopped

3 cups water

1. Heat a large soup pot over medium heat. Add the oil, garlic and onions and sauté for 5 minutes.

2. Season with salt and pepper.

3. Add the chicken broth and the potatoes and cook for 25 minutes until potatoes are soft.

4. Mash 2 of the potatoes; then add 3 cups water and season with additional salt and pepper. Add the cooked chorizo and diced potato and kale. Cook for 15 more minutes.

BUTTERNUT SQUASH SOUP ✺

Butternut squash is very versatile. It's especially good in soups, stews, risottos, and burritos. It's tasty, hearty, and healthy, and it lasts for weeks in a cool dark place before cooking.

MAKES 10 SERVINGS

1 large butternut squash (about 2 pounds)

3 tablespoons organic butter

1 small organic white onion, minced

1 celery stalk, diced

1 tablespoon freshly grated ginger (optional)

6 cups homemade or organic chicken broth

Kosher salt, to taste

Freshly ground black pepper, to taste

½ cup organic heavy cream

Pinch of freshly grated nutmeg, for garnish

Sour cream, for garnish

1. Preheat the oven to 350°F.

2. Cut the squash in half lengthwise and scoop out the seeds. Arrange the squash halves in a roasting pan that has been greased with olive oil or butter. Bake the squash in the oven for 40 to 45 minutes or until the flesh is very tender. Set aside to cool. When the squash is completely cool, scoop the flesh from the skin.

3. While the squash is baking, melt the butter in a saucepan over medium-low. Sauté the onion, celery, and ginger, if using, for 5 minutes or until the onion and celery are softened.

4. Add the chicken broth and simmer for 10 minutes, covered. Add the squash to the saucepan and cook for 2 to 3 more minutes.

5. Transfer the mixture to a blender or food processor, in batches, and purée until smooth. Add enough water to achieve the desired consistency. Season with salt and pepper to taste.

6. Return the soup to the saucepan, add the cream, and cook over medium until hot.

7. Garnish each serving with a heaping teaspoon of real sour cream and nutmeg.

ROASTED CAULIFLOWER SOUP ❧

PREP TIME: 5 MINUTES | COOK TIME: 25 MINUTES | READY IN: 30 MINUTES

Roasted cauliflower is a great base flavor for this creamy and delicious soup. I like to make this soup both in fall and spring.

MAKES 10 SERVINGS

1 tablespoon extra-virgin olive oil

½ cup diced carrot

½ cup roasted shallots (see note on page 218)

1 tablespoon herbes de Provence

4 cups roasted cauliflower (see 218)

4 cups low-sodium chicken broth

¼ cup organic heavy cream

Kosher salt, to taste

Freshly ground black pepper, to taste

1 teaspoon minced fresh chives

1. Heat the oil in a heavy soup pot over medium heat. Add the carrot, roasted shallots and herbes de Provence. Sauté for 5 minutes.

2. Add the cauliflower, chicken broth, and cream. Cook for 20 minutes.

3. Purée the soup with an immersion blender or in a food processor until smooth.

4. Season with salt and pepper. Garnish with fresh chives.

Chef's Note: The recipe video at HarvestEating.com demonstrates how to make a creamy and delicious soup from roasted cauliflower.

LEEK AND POTATO SOUP

PREP TIME: 10 MINUTES | COOK TIME: 25 MINUTES | READY IN: 35 MINUTES

This is a hearty and delicious soup with an incredible leek flavor and thick texture from the russet potatoes. When served with a grilled cheese sandwich, it is perfect for a cold fall day.

MAKES 6 SERVINGS

2 bunches fresh leeks, sliced (about 6 total)

2 garlic cloves, chopped

Pinch of kosher salt

Pinch of freshly ground black pepper

2 large russet potatoes, peeled and quartered

6 cups organic chicken broth

¾ cups organic cream

1. Sauté the leeks and garlic in a large heavy-bottomed pot or Dutch oven over medium heat. Season with salt and pepper.
2. Add the potatoes and chicken broth and simmer for 25 minutes.
3. Purée in the pot with an immersion blender or transfer to a food processor.
4. Adjust the seasoning and add the cream to the soup.

Chefs Note: To jazz the soup up when serving, garnish it with a dollop of crème fraîche and some crispy fried leeks!

ESCAROLE AND POTATO SOUP ❧

PREP TIME: 10 MINUTES | COOK TIME: 35 MINUTES | READY IN: 45 MINUTES

This soup is great for a cold night. The healthy escarole provides a slightly bitter taste that plays well with the hearty potato and rich chicken stock. Escarole can be found throughout the year, but is best in the early fall.

MAKES 10 SERVINGS

¼ cup extra-virgin olive oil

1 garlic clove, minced

1 medium onion, diced

1 small carrot, diced

1 celery stalk, diced

8 cups chicken broth

10 cups escarole

2 medium russet potatoes, diced

Kosher salt

Freshly ground black pepper

2 tablespoons grated Parmesan cheese

1. Heat the oil in a heavy-bottomed pot over medium heat. Add the garlic, onion, carrot, and celery and sauté for 5 minutes.

2. Add the chicken broth, escarole, and diced potatoes. Bring to boil, then reduce the heat to medium low and simmer for 30 minutes. Season the soup with the salt and pepper to taste; then add the Parmesan cheese.

BIBB LETTUCE AND ARUGULA SALAD ❋

PREP TIME: 15 MINUTES | READY IN: 15 MINUTES

This tasty salad is made with organic Bibb lettuce, tangy arugula, walnuts and organic Bosc pears. I make this salad with fresh greens from my garden. The sun-dried cherry vinaigrette gives a sweet flavor and goes well with the Saga blue cheese.

MAKES 4 SERVINGS

1 cup organic Bibb lettuce (torn)

1 cup organic arugula

3 tablespoons sun-dried cherry vinaigrette (page 221)

¼ cup walnuts

½ cup organic Bosc pear, sliced

2 tablespoons grated Saga blue cheese (nearly freeze before grating)

Pinch of freshly ground black pepper

1. Combine the lettuce and arugula in a large bowl.

2. Toss well with the vinaigrette, being careful not to damage the lettuce or arugula.

3. Add the walnuts and pear; then use a grater to "shower" the very cold blue cheese on top.

4. Season with black pepper and serve.

ARUGULA SALAD ✺

PREP TIME: 5 MINUTES | READY IN: 5 MINUTES

This salad is very balanced because the fat in the nuts and cheese is offset by the acidity of the vinegars. I think the peppery flavor of arugula really shines through in this salad.

MAKES 4 SERVINGS

2 bunches arugula

1 tablespoon balsamic vinegar

1 tablespoon red wine vinegar

5 tablespoons extra-virgin olive oil

Kosher salt, to taste

Freshly ground black pepper, to taste

¼ cup toasted pine nuts

Parmesan cheese

1. Wash and spin dry the arugula. Reserve in a salad bowl.

2. Make the vinaigrette by combining the vinegars and olive oil and whisking to emulsify. Season the greens with salt and pepper and toss gently with the vinaigrette. Add the toasted pine nuts.

3. Divide the salad among four plates. With your vegetable peeler, make long shavings of Parmesan and arrange on top of each salad. Drizzle a little extra balsamic vinegar over the cheese.

Chef's Note: Pine nuts can be lightly toasted on a baking sheet in a 250 degree oven for 10 minutes. Watch closely.

ASPARAGUS SALAD
WITH SESAME GINGER VINAIGRETTE ✱

PREP TIME: 5 MINUTES | COOK TIME: 5 MINUTES | READY IN: 10 MINUTES

This is a perfect way to showcase fresh spring asparagus. This salad is very easy to make. Be sure not to oversteam the asparagus; the stalks should retain some crispness or be al dente. When you remove them from the steamer, toss them in ice water to "shock" them and help maintain their green color and crispness.

MAKES 3 SERVINGS

1 pounds asparagus, steamed and cooled, cut into 1-inch pieces

¼ cup sliced carrot

3 tablespoons sesame ginger vinaigrette (page 226), divided

3 cups torn organic green leaf or other lettuce

Kosher salt, to taste

A few twists of freshly ground black pepper

Sesame seeds, for garnish

1. Toss the cooked asparagus and carrots in 1 tablespoon of the vinaigrette.

2. Add the lettuce, the rest of the sesame ginger vinaigrette, salt and pepper and toss gently.

3. Garnish with the sesame seeds.

ROMAINE SALAD WITH VALDEON BLUE CHEESE AND POMEGRANATES ❁

PREP TIME: 10 MINUTES | READY IN: 10 MINUTES

This recipe features a delightful French blue cheese and pomegranate seeds and is perfect with crunchy romaine lettuce. It makes a great dinner party salad. If Valdeon cheese is not available any good-quality blue cheese will work.

MAKES 4 SIDE OR 2 DINNER SALADS

1 bunch fresh hearts of romaine lettuce

1 ounce Valdeon blue cheese

½ cup sour cream

2 tablespoons cream

Pinch of kosher salt

Pinch of freshly ground black pepper

2 tablespoons pomegranate seeds

1. Carefully rinse the lettuce under cold water, then dry with a kitchen towel and arrange on chilled plates.

2. Combine the blue cheese, sour cream, cream, salt, and pepper in a bowl and mix well. Be sure to retain some chunks of the blue cheese in the dressing.

3. Dress the romaine leaves with the blue cheese dressing mixture and top with the pomegranate seeds.

Chef's Note: To remove the pomegranate seeds from the pod, you must first wash the fruit; then slice it in half. Holding it with the seeds facing you over a bowl of cold water, with your fingers or the tip of a butter knife, pluck the seeds out and let them sink to the bottom of the bowl. Don't worry about any pieces of the pod falling in. You can remove them later. Scoop the seeds out of the water with a small strainer.

GREEN LEAF SALAD
WITH LEMON-THYME VINAIGRETTE ☀

PREP TIME: 2 MINUTES | READY IN: 2 MINUTES

This makes a delicious light lunch salad with seasonal mixed baby greens and a lemon-thyme vinaigrette. I suggest pairing this with my chicken salad with tarragon and crème frâiche.

MAKES 2 CUPS

2 cups torn organic green leaf lettuce

2 tablespoons Lemon-Thyme Vinaigrette (page 224)

1. Toss the leaf lettuce with the vinaigrette and serve.

Chef's Note: See the recipe video for lemon-thyme vinaigrette in "vinaigrette recipes" section on HarvestEating.com.

SIMPLE AVOCADO SALAD ✳ ✳

Here is a simple recipe for making an avocado salad to serve alongside eggs, fish, or chicken and with tortilla chips, in quesadillas, or in burritos. I like to snack on these with organic blue corn tortilla chips.

MAKES 4 SERVINGS

2 Haas avocados

1 teaspoon chopped Italian flat leaf parsley or cilantro

2 ounces good feta cheese (optional)

Pinch of kosher salt or Fleur de sel

Freshly ground black pepper, to taste

2 tablespoons good extra-virgin olive oil

1. Slice the avocados carefully, cutting around the pit. Open the avocado, and remove the pit. Scoop out the flesh with a spoon and place in a bowl.

2. Add the parsley, feta, if using, salt, pepper, and oil and gently mix. Try not to break up the ingredients; we are not looking for mush. It should be chunky.

Chef's Note: Fleur de sel is the king of salts. It is the top layer that forms flowers on the waters surface in salt ponds. These "flowers" are then harvested and sold as fleur de sel.

CHOPPED ORIENTAL SALAD ☀

PREP TIME: 15 MINUTES | READY IN: 15 MINUTES

This crunchy Oriental salad is a sure hit. Crisp lettuces, peppers, asparagus and cabbage combine to make a complete meal with sesame grilled chicken. There is an explosion of flavor and texture in your mouth with every bite.

MAKES 4 SERVINGS

2 hearts of romaine, julienned

1 cup julienned carrot

1 cup chopped cabbage

¾ pound asparagus, grilled (page 97)

1 cup chopped bell pepper

½ cup chopped spring onions

2 tablespoons chopped fresh cilantro

1 cup diced grilled chicken

¼ cup sesame ginger vinaigrette (page 226)

1. Combine the romaine, carrot, cabbage, asparagus, pepper, onions, cilantro, and chicken in a large bowl.

2. Add the vinaigrette and toss all ingredients well.

Chef's Note: Be sure to use very fresh ingredients, local and organic if possible.

BIRD'S CILANTRO CHICKEN SALAD ☀

PREP TIME: 15 MINUTES | READY IN: 15 MINUTES

This is a recipe adapted from my sister Jackie, who I call "the Bird". It is a healthy, very light and tasty chicken salad that is easy to make in fifteen minutes or less. Marukan rice vinegar is available at most good grocery stores. If you can't find it, you may use another rice wine vinegar. The wonton skins are found in the freezer section.

MAKES 4 SERVINGS

4 cups shredded lettuce (romaine, iceberg, or a mixture)

1 cup chopped fresh cilantro

1 cup poached, cooled, and shredded chicken breast (about 1 breast)

½ cup salted whole cashews

¼ cup Marukan seasoned rice wine vinegar

1 teaspoon sesame oil

Fried wonton skins

1. Place four salad bowls in the refrigerator 20 minutes before serving.

2. Combine the lettuce, cilantro, chicken, and cashews in a large bowl.

3. Combine the rice wine vinegar and sesame oil and whisk together. Pour over the salad and gently mix.

4. Divide the salad among the four cold salad bowls and top each salad with some fried wonton skins.

Chef's Note: Make sure all ingredients are cold and fresh. This is a cooling salad and tastes much more refreshing with crisp lettuce and cold chicken.

MIXED GREEN SALAD ☀

PREP TIME: 5 MINUTES | READY IN: 5 MINUTES

I like to make simple salads for lunch with greens from my garden. Young lettuces are so much better than store-bought, factory-farm-produced jumbo heads. Learn how to create a delicious mixed green salad from the garden and enjoy it with pomegranate vinaigrette.

MAKES 2 SERVINGS

2 cups organic field greens

½ cup julienned organic carrot

3 tablespoons pomegranate vinaigrette (page 237)

Pinch of kosher salt (optional)

Pinch of black pepper (optional)

1 tablespoon grated Parmigiano-Reggiano cheese

1. Toss the washed and dried greens with the carrot and vinaigrette.

2. Season with salt and pepper, if using. Top the salad with the grated cheese.

CRUNCHY CABBAGE SALAD ✺ ❋

PREP TIME: 10 MINUTES | READY IN: 10 MINUTES

Here's a new twist when you're looking to fit a green salad onto your menu. This salad is very abundant in the texture department. To me it's perfect picnic food. Served cold, it can be very refreshing during hot months.

MAKES 6 SERVINGS

1 head savoy cabbage,
   shredded (about 6 cups)

1 cup seedless red grapes

2 large apples, chopped

1 tablespoon chopped pecans

3 tablespoons nonfat plain yogurt

1 tablespoon mayonnaise

Freshly ground black pepper,
   to taste

Pinch of curry powder

1. Place the cabbage in a large bowl. Add the grapes, apples, and pecans.

2. In a small bowl, mix the yogurt, mayonnaise, pepper, and curry powder. Add to the salad and toss.

OMI'S CABBAGE SLAW ✲

PREP TIME: 2 HOURS, 5 MINUTES | READY IN: 2 HOURS, 5 MINUTES

My mother-in-law Elisabeth is a feisty Bavarian woman who has inspired my cooking from the day I first tried her food. The simple and perfectly executed flavors of her food are always on my mind. This dish has become a family staple at our house, year-round. Every time I make this dish somebody asks for the recipe.

MAKES 15 SERVINGS

1 head cabbage, julienned

1 teaspoon kosher salt

4 tablespoons apple cider vinegar

3 tablespoons pure olive oil

½ teaspoon freshly ground black
   pepper

1. Place the cabbage in a large bowl. Add the kosher salt and toss. Add the cider vinegar, olive oil, and black pepper.

2. Allow to marinate for 2 hours at room temperature. The cabbage will soften in texture.

BOSC PEAR AND FIELD GREENS
SALAB WITH BALSAMIC REDUCTION ❄ ✳

PREP TIME: 10 MINUTES | COOK TIME: 5 MINUTES | READY IN: 15 MINUTES

This salad is simple to prepare and elegant. Bosc pears are firm and sweet and go well with the cheese. The syrupy balsamic vinegar makes a super finishing touch and the walnuts add a significant nutritional punch.

MAKES 2 SERVINGS

1 ripe Bosc pear

2 cups field greens

3 tablespoons Harvest Eating
   French Vinaigrette (page 271)

Kosher salt, to taste

Freshly ground black pepper,
   to taste

½ ounce feta cheese

¼ cup chopped walnuts

1 tablespoon local honey

1 tablespoon balsamic vinegar
   reduction (page 270)

1. Slice the pear and remove the seed pocket and stem rib; set aside.

2. Dress the greens with the French vinaigrette and season with salt and pepper.

3. Divide the greens between two serving plates. Top each with the sliced pear, feta cheese, and walnuts and drizzle each plate with the honey and balsamic reduction.

ROASTED BEET SALAD
WITH SHEEP'S MILK FETA CHEESE ✽

This delicious salad features sweet roasted beets, simply treated with olive oil, salt and pepper, then tossed in a mustard vinaigrette. This salad has great color and texture.

MAKES 2 SERVINGS

1 whole organic red or golden beet

2 tablespoons olive oil

Kosher salt, to taste

Freshly ground black pepper, to taste

1 cup torn organic green leaf lettuce

2 tablespoons Harvest Eating French Vinaigrette (page 271)

⅛ cup sheep's milk feta cheese

1. Preheat the oven to 375°F.

2. Toss the beet in olive oil, salt, and pepper. Place in a roasting pan and roast for 30 minutes, or until the beet is tender. Remove from the oven and let cool. When cool, peel the beet and cut it into small cubes.

3. Toss the lettuce with the French vinaigrette and season to taste with salt and pepper.

4. Serve the lettuce divided between two plates and top with the beet and crumbled feta cheese.

BAVARIAN POTATO SALAD 🍁

PREP TIME: 10 MINUTES | MARINATING TIME: 1 HOUR | COOK TIME: 20 MINUTES | READY IN: 1½ HOURS

This recipe for a German style potato salad is my mother-in-law's recipe, we call her Omi. This recipe is always the star of any party, picnic, or meal it is a part of. Simple flavors make this a great recipe that will become a family favorite for sure.

MAKES 8 SERVINGS

10 medium red-skinned potatoes

1 bunch fresh chives, minced
(about ¼ cup)

¼ cup apple cider vinegar

½ cup pure or light olive oil

Kosher salt, to taste

Freshly ground black pepper,
to taste

1. Place the potatoes in a steamer, leaving the skins on. Steam over boiling water until just fork tender. Check them at 20 minutes. Over-cooking the potatoes at this step will require that you start over. They cannot be too soft.

2. When the potatoes yield slightly to the fork, turn off the heat. Remove the steamer basket and allow to cool on a cutting board for 1 hour.

3. When cool, remove the skins and slice the potatoes into ¼-inch-thick slices. Some will break which is okay.

4. Place the potatoes in a nonreactive bowl (ceramic is best) then add the chives, vinegar, oil, salt and pepper. Toss well.

5. Let the potatoes marinate at room temperature for 1 hour (longer if you have time), tossing every 30 minutes.

Chef's Note: Omi uses a spice mix called Aromat, by Knorr. It is sold in a little yellow spice container. It does add a special flavor but contains MSG, so I prefer to omit it. She also uses corn oil in the recipe, but I replace it with light olive oil.

6 | SIDES

MUSHROOM SAUTÉ ✳

Mushrooms can really bring a gourmet touch to foods they're paired with. I often hunt for mushrooms on my farm in late spring to make this dish. The finished mushrooms are great on pasta, on pizza, in soups, or on grilled meat like steak and chicken. As an option, two tablespoons of heavy cream can be added with the thyme to create a delicious mouthfeel.

MAKES 4 SERVINGS

1 tablespoon olive oil

½ stick butter

4 cups sliced wild mushrooms, such as chanterelles

¼ teaspoon salt

¼ teaspoon freshly ground black pepper

1 whole shallot, sliced

1 garlic clove, minced

½ cup dry white wine

1 tablespoon chopped fresh thyme

1. Heat the oil and butter in a stainless steel skillet over medium-high heat. Add the mushrooms and stir well.

2. Season with salt and pepper. Continue cooking until the mushrooms start to brown a bit; then add the shallot and garlic.

3. Cook for another minute. Deglaze the pan with the wine. Cook until the wine evaporates.

4. Add the thyme and stir.

5. Serve the mushrooms on pasta or crisp bread.

CURRIED SWEET PEA SAUTÉ ✳

PREP TIME: 10 MINUTES | COOK TIME: 15 MINUTES | READY IN: 25 MINUTES

Need a simple and delicious way to use up abundant spring peas? Here it is. It takes no time to produce this Indian-inspired side dish with a hint of curry and a touch of cream.

MAKES 2 SERVINGS

1¼ cups fresh local peas

1 tablespoon organic unsalted butter

2 tablespoons minced shallot

1 garlic clove, minced

1 teaspoon curry powder

1 tablespoon organic heavy cream

Kosher salt, to taste

Freshly ground black pepper, to taste

1. Blanch the peas in salted boiling water for 8 to 10 minutes. Drain and shock in an ice water bath.

2. Heat the butter in a sauté pan over medium heat. Add the shallot, garlic, curry, and cream and cook for 2 minutes.

3. Add the blanched peas and cook for 3 minutes.

4. Season with the salt and pepper.

Chef's Note: Frozen peas can be used when fresh are not in season. This same recipe can be made all summer long with snap beans or broccoli.

GRILLED ASPARAGUS ✳

PREP TIME: 2 MINUTES | COOK TIME: 8 MINUTES | READY IN: 10 MINUTES

Tired of boiled asparagus? Try this simple grilled asparagus; it becomes like candy when grilled. This dish is frequently served at my house in springtime when local asparagus are in season. I like using very thin asparagus for this dish.

MAKES 6 SERVINGS

¾ pound local thin asparagus

3 tablespoons extra-virgin olive oil

Pinch of kosher salt

Pinch of freshly ground black pepper

1. Clean and preheat the grill to medium hot.

2. Toss the asparagus in a bowl with the oil, salt and pepper.

3. Place the asparagus spears on the grill.

4. Cook for 4 to 5 minutes on the first side. Carefully turn them and cook for another 3 minutes.

KALE GREENS ✳

PREP TIME: 5 MINUTES | COOK TIME: 35 MINUTES | READY IN: 40 MINUTES

Kale is similar to collards, but, in my opinion, it tastes milder. I find my kids prefer slow-cooked kale over collard greens. Kale is loaded with nutrition as well. Try this green the next time you have a meat dish; the slightly bitter taste helps to balance out heavy dishes.

MAKES 10 SERVINGS

2 tablespoons pure olive oil

1 small shallot, sliced

1 garlic clove, minced

1 pound fresh kale

1 quart organic chicken broth

Pinch of kosher salt

Pinch of freshly ground black pepper

1. Combine the oil, shallot, and garlic in a large Dutch oven or stockpot over medium-high heat. Sauté for 2 minutes.

2. Add the kale, chicken broth, salt, and pepper.

3. Reduce the heat to medium low, cover, and cook for 35 to 40 minutes.

Chef's Note: Use the same recipe for mustard greens, Swiss chard, rainbow chard, or beet greens.

BROCCOLI STIR-FRY ✳

PREP TIME: 5 MINUTES | COOK TIME: 6 MINUTES | READY IN: 11 MINUTES

Stir-frying is a well-known technique for cooking broccoli and other vegetables and requires high heat and flavorful ingredients. It's perfect over aromatic rice such as basmati or jasmine.

MAKES 3 SERVINGS

1 tablespoon pure olive oil

1 tablespoon minced fresh ginger

1 garlic clove, minced

3 cups broccoli florets, steamed

1 tablespoon toasted sesame oil

1 tablespoon low-sodium soy sauce

Pinch of kosher salt

Pinch of freshly ground black pepper

1. Heat the olive oil in a wok over medium-high heat until a drop of water pops in the oil.

2. Add the ginger, garlic, and broccoli florets. Stir-fry for a few minutes; then add the sesame oil and soy sauce.

3. Stir-fry for 2 minutes and season with salt and pepper.

WILD MUSHROOM RISOTTO ✳

PREP TIME: 10 MINUTES | COOK TIME: 30 MINUTES | READY IN: 40 MINUTES

Learn the proper technique to make a delicious, creamy risotto. A risotto can include many seasonal varieties of produce. This one features wild mushrooms and fresh thyme.

MAKES 10 SERVINGS

- 4 tablespoons extra-virgin olive oil, divided
- 3 tablespoons organic unsalted butter, divided
- ½ cup minced organic white onion, divided
- 2 garlic cloves, minced and divided
- 2 cups assorted wild mushrooms
- Kosher salt, to taste
- Freshly ground black pepper, to taste
- 3 tablespoons minced fresh thyme, divided
- 2 cups aborio rice, uncooked
- 6 to 8 cups hot chicken broth
- ½ cup dry white wine
- 2 tablespoons grated Romano cheese

1. Heat a heavy Dutch oven over medium heat. Add 1 tablespoon of the oil, 1 tablespoon of the butter, 1 tablespoon of the onion, and half the garlic. Sauté for 1 or 2 minutes; then add the mushrooms. Season with salt and pepper.

2. Continue cooking until the mushrooms have softened and begun to caramelize. Add 1 tablespoon of the fresh thyme and stir.

3. Remove the mushroom mixture from the pan and set aside.

4. Add the remaining oil, butter, onion, and garlic to the pan and sauté for 2 minutes. Then add the rice. Stir very well and cook for 1 to 2 minutes. Add wine and cook until dry. Begin adding the broth a ladleful at a time.

5. Continue to add broth by the ladleful, allowing each addition to be absorbed before adding the next, and cook until the rice is creamy but still al dente or still slightly firm.

6. Turn off the heat. Add half of the cheese and stir.

7. When serving the risotto, top with the mushrooms, the remaining cheese, thyme and a touch of olive oil.

Chef's Note: As I mentioned, risotto can be used with many different seasonal vegetables and also with protein such as shrimp, scallops, shellfish and fish.

CABBAGE SAUTÉ ✳

PREP TIME: 5 MINUTES | COOK TIME: 4 MINUTES | READY IN: 9 MINUTES

This simple recipe for a quick cabbage sauté is loaded with flavor. Crunchy cabbage and tangy mustard seeds make this a tasty side dish for grilled pork or chicken. I often use it as a side with a spicy, yogurt-marinated tandoori chicken.

MAKES 4 SERVINGS

2 teaspoons organic butter

½ cup diced organic white onion

1 tablespoon yellow or brown whole mustard seeds

2 cups shredded cabbage (about ½ head)

Kosher salt, to taste

Freshly ground black pepper, to taste

1. Heat the butter in a large skillet over medium-high heat. Add the onion and mustard seed and sauté for 30 seconds.

2. Add the shredded cabbage, salt, and pepper and sauté for about 4 minutes.

3. Serve next to your favorite pork or chicken dish.

COLLARD GREENS ✳

This simple recipe produces tender and flavorful greens that make a hearty meal on their own, or a great side dish. Collards are easy to grow at home. They like cold weather and produce a nice crop with a minimal effort. We grow them in early spring and late fall on the farm.

MAKES 6 SERVINGS

2 tablespoons olive oil

½ cup chopped organic white onion

1 teaspoon kosher salt

¼ teaspoon freshly ground black pepper

2 pounds organic washed collard greens

2½ cups organic chicken broth

1. Heat the olive oil in a large, heavy pot over medium heat. Add the onion and cook for 2 minutes, stirring often.

2. Season with the salt and pepper.

3. Add the collard greens and chicken broth.

4. Reduce the heat to low, cover tightly, and cook for 45 minutes.

CREAMED SPINACH ✹

PREP TIME: 10 MINUTES | COOK TIME: 25 MINUTES | READY IN: 35 MINUTES

Here is a hearty recipe for cooking spinach that is comforting and goes well with a juicy steak. I prefer using savoy spinach, which has dark green leaves that are crinkly and curly. This more rustic variety of spinach is much better then baby spinach in my opinion.

MAKES 6 SERVINGS

2 tablespoons olive oil

½ cup minced onion

2 garlic cloves, minced

2 pounds savoy spinach, steamed

½ cup organic heavy cream

½ pound organic cream cheese

⅛ teaspoon freshly grated nutmeg

⅛ teaspoon kosher salt

⅛ teaspoon freshly ground black pepper

1. Heat the olive oil in a saucepan over medium heat. Add the onion and sauté for 2 minutes.

2. Add the garlic and sauté for 1 minute.

3. Add the spinach, cream, cream cheese, nutmeg, salt, and pepper and stir well.

4. Reduce the heat to low and cook for 20 minutes.

Chef's Note: To steam the spinach, place it in a perforated pot or steamer with a little water. Cover and steam for about 10 minutes. Run it under cold water to stop the cooking process. Let it drain and set aside.

GARLIC BROCCOLI ✳

PREP TIME: 2 MINUTES | COOK TIME: 5 MINUTES | READY IN: 7 MINUTES

If you use pre-cooked broccoli, this is a nice and easy way to prepare broccoli that can be on the table in five minutes. My kids love this recipe.

MAKES 6 SERVINGS

3 tablespoons clarified butter (page 31)

3 garlic cloves, minced

6 cups steamed fresh broccoli florets

2 tablespoons organic butter

Kosher salt, to taste

Freshly ground black pepper, to taste

1. Heat the clarified butter in a skillet over medium-low heat.

2. Add the garlic and cook, stirring frequently, for 2 minutes. Do not brown.

3. Add the steamed broccoli and butter to the skillet. Toss well to heat the florets and coat them with the butter.

4. Season with salt and pepper.

Chef's Note: We often take 2 whole stalks of fresh broccoli, portioned into florets, steam them for 5 to 7 minutes, and submerse them in an ice bath to stop the cooking process. We store them in the refrigerator or freezer for later use in salads or pastas or other dishes.

GARLIC SPINACH SAUTÉ ✳

PREP TIME: 5 MINUTES | COOK TIME: 5 MINUTES | READY IN: 10 MINUTES

This is a simple, flavorful side dish. I use Savoy spinach that grows in raised beds in both the spring and fall on our farm. It takes only ten minutes to make this dish so it's perfect for quick mid-week meals, and it's terrific with grilled fish.

MAKES 8 SERVING

3 tablespoons extra-virgin olive oil

2 garlic cloves, minced

10 cups fresh spinach, baby or large leaf

Pinch of kosher salt

Pinch of freshly ground black pepper

1. Heat the oil in a large pot or sauté pan over medium heat. Sauté the garlic for 30 seconds. Reduce the heat to low and add the spinach all at once.

2. Toss the spinach until it is wilted. Season with salt and pepper and serve.

Chefs Note: This is great in pasta, under grilled chicken, in wraps, on top of rice, or straight up as a side dish.

SESAME KALE ✳

PREP TIME: 10 MINUTES | COOK TIME: 15 MINUTES | READY IN: 25 MINUTES

Previously cooked kale makes a comeback in this simple yet tasty Asian-inspired dish. A touch of soy sauce, shallots, sesame oil, and sesame seeds provide the Asian flavors we all love.

MAKES 4 SERVINGS

2 pounds kale (3 cups steamed)

3 tablespoons low-sodium soy sauce

2 teaspoons black and white sesame seeds

2 tablespoons light or pure olive oil

1 medium shallot, sliced

2 teaspoons toasted sesame oil

1. Steam the kale in a stove-top steamer for about 10 minutes. Then, run the kale under cold water to stop the cooking process. Let it drain and set aside.

2. Heat the olive oil in a wok or sauté pan over medium heat.

3. Add the shallot and sauté for 1 minute. Add the steamed kale and stir-fry for 1 minute.

4. Add the soy sauce, sesame oil and sesame seeds and stir-fry for 1 minute longer.

ROASTED CORN CAKES ☀

PREP TIME: 10 MINUTES | COOK TIME: 10 MINUTES | READY IN: 20 MINUTES

A delicious way to use fresh, roasted summer corn is to learn how to make these roasted corn cakes, also known as "Johnny Cakes."

MAKES 4 SERVINGS

2 large free-range eggs

1 tablespoon granulated sugar

½ cup organic whole milk, plus more for thinning the batter, if necessary

¼ teaspoon baking powder

1 cup stone-ground cornmeal

½ cup all-purpose flour

1 cup roasted corn kernels, (kernels from 1 to 2 ears)

¼ teaspoon kosher salt

4 tablespoons organic unsalted butter, divided

1. Crack the eggs into a work bowl and add the sugar. Lightly beat them together.

2. Add ½ cup of the milk and the baking powder. Slowly add the cornmeal and whisk to combine.

3. Slowly whisk in the flour. Add additional milk if needed to create thick pourable batter.

4. Fold the roasted corn kernels into the batter. Season with the salt.

5. Heat a nonstick skillet and 1 tablespoon butter over medium heat. Add ¼ cup of batter and cook, turning once, until golden brown on both sides.

6. Repeat with all batter.

SPINACH AND CHEDDAR CHEESE STUFFED TOMATOES ☀

PREP TIME: 10 MINUTES | COOK TIME: 25 MINUTES | READY IN: 35 MINUTES

Here is a delicious way to use some of your fresh summer tomatoes: roasted in an oven, stuffed with spinach and topped with cheddar cheese.

MAKES 3 SERVINGS

3 beefsteak tomatoes

Kosher salt, to taste

Freshly ground black pepper, to taste

1 cup steamed fresh spinach

2 tablespoons grated Parmesan cheese

½ cup sharp cheddar cheese

1 tablespoon extra-virgin olive oil

1. Preheat the oven to 350°F.

2. Cut off the tops of the tomatoes and carefully scoop out the flesh, seeds and pulp.

3. Season the tomato cavity with salt and pepper.

4. Toss the spinach in a bowl with the Parmesan cheese and season with additional salt and pepper.

5. Carefully stuff the tomatoes with the spinach mixture and top with the cheddar cheese.

6. Drizzle a small amount of extra-virgin olive oil on top of the cheddar cheese. Place on a baking sheet in the oven to cook, about 15 minutes.

7. Check them often as the cheese can burn easily. You want them just golden brown.

Chef's Note: These spinach-stuffed tomatoes can be topped with jumbo lump crabmeat or even lobster.

TOMATO PIE ☀

PREP TIME: 20 MINUTES | COOK TIME: 45 MINUTES | READY IN: 65 MINUTES

This recipe is a delicious tomato pie from scratch—homemade pastry dough topped with organic heirloom tomatoes, applewood smoked bacon, fresh rosemary, and Spanish blue cheese.

MAKES 10 SERVINGS

1 recipe Pastry Dough (page 288)

2 large heirloom tomatoes, sliced, excess liquid removed

2 to 3 tablespoons extra-virgin olive oil

1 tablespoon chopped fresh rosemary

½ cup chopped, cooked applewood bacon

Kosher salt, to taste

Freshly ground black pepper, to taste

2 tablespoons blue cheese

3 tablespoons grated Parmesan cheese

1. Preheat the oven to 350°F.

2. Roll out the pie dough and press it into a greased tart pan. Prick the dough all over with a fork. Blind bake it for 10 to 15 minutes or until it is just starting to become golden brown. Remove from the oven.

3. Lay the tomato slices in the baked pie crust. Drizzle the olive oil over the tomatoes. Add the chopped rosemary and top with the bacon. Season with salt and pepper.

4. Shave the blue cheese over the bacon and add the Parmesan cheese.

5. Bake for 25 minutes or until the cheese starts to brown.

Chef's Note: This tomato pie is the perfect way to use abundant beef steak or heirloom tomatoes. Tomato pie is an elegant appetizer that is perfect for summer picnics.

TOMATOES WITH MIGNONETTE SAUCE ☀

PREP TIME: 10 MINUTES | MARINATING TIME: 30 MINUTES | READY IN: 40 MINUTES

This tomato recipe merges the freshness of seasonal tomatoes with a classical French sauce recipe. The herbs and tomatoes must be of high quality, preferably organic and very fresh. This is a go-to recipe to use up an abundant amount of herbs and tomatoes in late summer on our farm.

MAKES 4 SERVINGS

1 to 3 ripe tomatoes, beefsteak, Better Boy or Heirloom variety, sliced ¼-inch thick

1 shallot, finely minced

½ cup good-quality red wine or champagne vinegar

1 tablespoon minced fresh tarragon or basil

Pinch of kosher salt

A few twists of freshly ground black or white pepper

1. Combine the tomatoes, shallots, vinegar, tarragon, salt, and pepper in a nonreactive bowl. Marinate for 30 minutes.

2. Arrange the tomatoes on a serving platter.

3. Spoon the leftover marinade over the tomatoes.

Chef's Note: The addition of freshly grated Parmigiano-Reggiano cheese is nice if you're in the mood for the extra flavor boost.

CILANTRO AND TOMATO RICE ☀

PREP TIME: 15 MINUTES | COOK TIME: 50 MINUTES | READY IN: 65 MINUTES

Add great flavor and texture to your rice with this recipe. The addition of flavorful tomatoes, chickpeas, and almonds makes this rice dish a perfect accompaniment to grilled fish, chicken, or even beef.

MAKES 6 SERVINGS

1 cup short-grain brown rice

2 cups water

½ teaspoon salt, divided

1 pound fresh tomatoes, chopped

⅓ cup fresh cilantro

1 tablespoon extra-virgin olive oil

1 tablespoon lime juice or
   lemon juice

1 medium garlic clove, minced

1 teaspoon ground cumin

¼ teaspoon freshly ground
   black pepper

1 (14-ounce) can chickpeas,
   rinsed and drained

¼ cup slivered almonds

1. Place the rice, water, and ¼ teaspoon of the salt in a medium saucepan. Bring to a boil over high heat.

2. Reduce the heat to low, cover, and simmer for 45 minutes, or until the rice is tender and the liquid is absorbed.

3. Meanwhile, in a medium bowl, combine the tomatoes, cilantro, oil, lime juice or lemon juice, garlic, cumin, pepper, and the remaining ¼ teaspoon salt. Cover and let stand at room temperature.

4. Stir the cooked rice and chickpeas into the tomato mixture and top with the almonds.

CONFETTI RICE ☀

PREP TIME: 5 MINUTES | COOK TIME: 18 MINUTES | READY IN: 23 MINUTES

This is a great way to use up seasonal vegetables and bring extra flavor, color, and nutrition to white rice. Served molded, this looks great on a plate.

MAKES 6 SERVINGS

2 tablespoons organic unsalted butter

1 tablespoon chopped red onion

¼ cup diced zucchini

¼ cup diced red bell pepper

¼ cup diced carrots

1 teaspoon kosher salt

½ teaspoon freshly ground black pepper

1 cup uncooked rice

1½ cups water

1. Melt the butter in a saucepan over medium-low heat.

2. Add the onion, zucchini, bell pepper and carrot to the pan and season with salt and pepper. Stir to coat the vegetables well.

3. Add the rice and the water. Stir to combine.

4. Cover with a tight lid and bring the mixture to a simmer over medium heat.

5. Reduce the heat to low and simmer 15 minutes.

Chef's Note: Seasonal vegetables may be substituted for the zucchini and bell pepper.

CORN AND SHALLOT SAUTÉ ☀

PREP TIME: 10 MINUTES | COOK TIME: 15 MINUTES | READY IN: 25 MINUTES

This dish is a snap to make. It pairs very well with many summer foods like fish, steak, chicken, or as a vegetarian meal. I prefer to use a sweet corn, such as butter and sugar or Silver Queen variety.

MAKES 4 SERVINGS

2 teaspoons pure olive oil

1 teaspoon bacon fat (optional)

1 shallot, sliced

2 ears corn on the cob, remove kernels

2 tablespoons diced tomato

2 tablespoons heavy cream

Kosher salt, to taste

A few twists of freshly ground black pepper

1 teaspoon chopped fresh thyme

1. In a skillet over medium-high heat, combine the oil and bacon fat, if using. When hot, add the shallot and sauté for 30 seconds; then add the corn and sauté for 30 more seconds.

2. Add the tomato, cream, salt, and pepper and cook for a few minutes more until the cream is reduced by one-third.

3. Stir in the thyme and serve.

OVEN-DRIED TOMATOES ☀

PREP TIME: 25 MINUTES | COOK TIME: 2 HOURS | READY IN: 2 HOURS, 25 MINUTES

Oven-dried tomatoes packed in olive oil are a great way to use up your abundant summer tomatoes! Our youngest daughter, Ava, is an eating machine, but even she can't take care of all of them. This recipe makes enough for me to be able to store some in the fridge to use on bread and pizzas and in pasta dishes. I make these every week and always use them up. They only keep about one week.

MAKES 20 SERVINGS

20 organic or garden fresh Roma tomatoes

1 large bunch fresh thyme (about 12 sprigs)

Kosher salt, to taste

Freshly ground black pepper, to taste

Garlic pepper or herbes de Provence, to taste (optional)

Extra-virgin olive oil

1. Preheat the oven to 200°F.

2. Cut tomatoes in half and squeeze out the juice and seeds. Arrange cut side up on baking sheet that has been covered in foil.

3. Season the tomatoes with thyme, salt, pepper and garlic pepper or herbes de Provence.

4. Drizzle them with the olive oil and roast in the oven for at least 2 hours.

Chef's Note: This may take longer depending on the type of tomatoes, the size of your oven, etc. The tomatoes should shrink considerably and become very wrinkled. Also, these should be kept in a sterile jar in the refrigerator. They are NOT shelf stable.

OVEN-ROASTED CHERRY TOMATOES ☀

PREP TIME: 5 MINUTES | COOK TIME: 25 MINUTES | READY IN: 30 MINUTES

Learn how to oven-roast your crop of summer cherry tomatoes. Roasted with olive oil and fresh rosemary, these delicious cherry tomatoes are great in soups, pastas, and as a topping for Italian breads.

MAKES 10 SERVINGS

3½ cups ripe cherry tomatoes, halved

2 tablespoons extra-virgin olive oil

Kosher salt, to taste

A few twists of freshly ground black pepper

1 bunch fresh rosemary leaves (about 3 to 4 tablespoons)

1. Preheat the oven to 375°F.

2. Place the cherry tomatoes in a bowl and pour the extra-virgin olive oil on them. Season them with salt and pepper and mix well.

3. Spread the tomatoes in an even layer on a sheet pan.

4. Toss the rosemary leaves on the tomatoes.

5. Place in the hot oven for 20 to 25 minutes or until some roast marks develop. Be careful not to burn.

ROASTED LOCAL SWEET CORN ☀

PREP TIME: 5 MINUTES | COOK TIME: 30 MINUTES | READY IN: 35 MINUTES

A simple and delicious method of preparing local abundant corn, roasting brings out the caramel flavor and sweetness. Look for local corn such as silver queen or butter and sugar corn, which are both yellow and white. I often make flavored butters to serve with roasted corn such as: parsley-garlic, basil-cheese, or cilantro-lime.

MAKES 4 SERVINGS

5 ears local sweet corn, husked and silks removed

⅛ cup pure olive oil

¼ teaspoon kosher salt

⅛ teaspoon freshly ground black pepper

Pinch of chili powder (optional)

1. Preheat the oven to 375°F.

2. Combine the corn, oil, salt, pepper, and chili powder in a large plastic bag and gently shake to coat.

3. Place the corn in a roasting dish and cook in the oven until the ears begin to get some color, about 15 minutes.

4. Enjoy on the cob or remove the kernels and use for salads, cornbread, or sautéed dishes like pasta.

Chef's Note: You can use any spice you like, such as herbs de Provence or garlic powder, to season the corn.

SESAME CUCUMBERS ☀

PREP TIME: 5 MINUTES | MARINATING TIME: 25 MINUTES | READY IN: 30 MINUTES

This simple and healthy side dish is easy to make and very light and delicious. It makes a good snack while sitting on the front porch on hot summer afternoons.

MAKES 6 SERVINGS

2 cups thinly sliced cucumbers
(about 2 cucumbers)

2 tablespoons seasoned rice
wine vinegar

1 tablespoon toasted sesame oil

1 tablespoon toasted sesame
seeds (optional)

1 tablespoon minced fresh
cilantro (optional)

1 drop sriracha chili sauce
(optional)

1. Place the cucumbers in a nonreactive bowl. Add the vinegar, oil, and sesame seeds, if using.

2. Add the cilantro and chili sauce, if using. Marinate for 25 minutes.

3. Serve cold or at room temperature.

SWEET CORN SAUTÉ ☀

PREP TIME: 10 MINUTES | COOK TIME: 10 MINUTES | READY IN: 20 MINUTES

This recipe is perfect to combat the aggressive summer inventory we gardeners have. It's a delicious way to prepare your fresh summer corn with zucchini and tomatoes.

MAKES 4 SERVINGS

2 tablespoons organic unsalted butter

1 tablespoon extra-virgin olive oil

½ cup minced organic white onion

½ cup minced zucchini

1 garlic clove, minced

Kosher salt, to taste

Freshly ground black pepper, to taste

¼ cup minced tomato

2 cups sweet corn, removed from cob

1 tablespoon chopped fresh basil

1. Add the butter and olive oil to a pan over medium-high heat.

2. Add the onion, zucchini, and garlic to the pan. Season with salt and pepper and stir.

3. Add the tomato and corn. Reseason with pinches of salt and pepper to taste.

4. Cook until the corn caramelizes slightly, 5 to 10 minutes. Add the basil and serve.

GREEN BEANS WITH SHALLOTS AND CREAM ✤

PREP TIME: 10 MINUTES | COOK TIME: 20 MINUTES | READY IN: 30 MINUTES

Green beans really come to life with sautéed shallots and a touch of cream. This recipe can be served with any protein and is a favorite for the holiday table.

MAKES 4 SERVINGS

1 pound fresh green beans

1 tablespoon extra-virgin olive oil

½ shallot, sliced

1 tablespoon organic heavy cream

1 tablespoon organic unsalted butter

¼ cup vegetable broth or chicken broth

Pinch of kosher salt

Pinch of freshly ground black pepper

1. Bring a large pot of heavily salted water (about 2 gallons) to a boil over high heat. Add the beans and cook for 10 minutes. Drain the beans and place them in an ice bath to stop the cooking process.

2. Heat the oil in a skillet over medium-high heat. When it's hot, add the shallot and cook for 1 minute. Add the cream, butter, broth, and beans.

3. Cook for 5 to 6 minutes, tossing the beans in the sauce and allowing the sauce to reduce just a bit.

4. Season with salt and pepper.

AU GRATIN POTATOES ✳

PREP TIME: 25 MINUTES | COOK TIME: 45 MINUTES | READY IN: 70 MINUTES

The classic baked potato dish made with thinly sliced Yukon Gold potatoes, an infused milk mixture with garlic, butter and fresh herbs combine to make this dish a holiday classic.

MAKES 10 SERVINGS

2 pounds russet potatoes, peeled and thinly sliced

1¼ cups organic heavy cream

¾ cups organic whole milk

⅛ teaspoon freshly grated nutmeg

2 cups shredded sharp cheddar or Gruyère cheese

Freshly ground black pepper, to taste

Kosher salt, to taste

1. Using a mandoline, slice the potatoes as thin as you can. Put the potato slices in a water bath to keep them from oxidizing or turning brown.

2. Dry the potatoes in a kitchen towel before assembly.

3. Preheat the oven to 350°F.

4. Combine the cream, milk and nutmeg in a bowl and stir to mix.

3. Layer the potatoes, cheese, and seasoned milk in a heavy-bottomed 2-quart baking dish until full.

4. Season each layer with pepper and salt.

5. Bake for 45 minutes or until bubbly and starting to brown and potatoes become tender.

Chef's Note: Let the potatoes cool for 8 minutes before serving for optimal eating enjoyment.

ROASTED CAULIFLOWER ✶

PREP TIME: 2 MINUTES | COOK TIME: 15 MINUTES | READY IN: 17 MINUTES

Roasted cauliflower is very versatile; it can be eaten as a side dish, tossed in soup on salads or even in risotto. The roasting really improves the flavor of the cauliflower.

MAKES 6 SERVINGS

5 cups cauliflower florets

5 tablespoons extra-virgin olive oil

1 teaspoon kosher salt

1 tablespoon freshly ground
    black pepper

1. Preheat the oven to 375°F.

2. Toss the cauliflower in a bowl with the olive oil, salt, and pepper.

3. Place in a roasting dish and cook until the cauliflower begins to brown slightly, about 15 minutes.

Chef's Note: The roasted flavor of the cauliflower makes many dishes special such as cauliflower soup, fresh salads, pizza, or mashed cauliflower.

CORNBREAD STUFFING ❋

PREP TIME: 25 MINUTES | COOK TIME: 60 MINUTES | READY IN: 85 MINUTES

In the South we call it dressing. Growing up in northern New Jersey, we called it stuffing, and it was stuffed into the bird. Here it is cooked in a dish. Either way it rocks. The sausage is amazing here and the bell pepper background flavor is really nice.

MAKES 10 SERVINGS

Yellow or red cornbread mix

2 tablespoons extra-virgin olive oil, divided

1 cup chopped celery

1½ cups chopped onion

1 cup chopped carrots

1 cup chopped green bell pepper

Kosher salt, to taste

Freshly ground black pepper, to taste

1 medium sweet Italian sausage, chopped (optional)

1 medium spicy Italian sausage, chopped (optional)

1 medium unpeeled tart apple, chopped

3 cups chopped cremini mushrooms

¼ cup sherry

3½ tablespoons chopped fresh sage

2 cups organic low-sodium chicken broth

1. Preheat the oven to 350°F.

2. Make the cornbread according to package instructions. Set aside.

3. Heat 1 tablespoon of the olive oil in a sauté pan over medium-high heat. Add the celery, onion, carrots, and bell pepper. Season with salt and pepper and stir to combine.

4. Add the sausages, if using. Sauté until the sausage is cooked and broken down and the vegetables are soft.

5. Reduce the heat to medium. Add the chopped apple and cook about 5 minutes more.

6. Carefully remove the mixture to a large work bowl.

7. Using the same sauté pan, add the remaining olive oil and the cremini mushrooms. Season them with additional salt and pepper. Cook over medium-low heat until the mushrooms cook down, 8 to 10 minutes.

8. Turn off the heat and deglaze the pan with the sherry. Turn the heat back to medium and scrape up the bits of mushroom on the bottom of the pan. The sherry will darken and boil, flavoring the mushrooms.

9. Add the mushrooms and liquid to the mixture in the work bowl. Add the fresh sage. Stir to combine.

10. Break up the prepared cornbread by hand into small pieces and add it to the mixture. Stir to combine.

Moisten the mixture with the chicken broth. Season it liberally with additional salt and pepper.

11. Place the mixture in a large greased casserole dish and bake for 40 minutes.

Chef's Note: This dressing could be either moist or dry, adjust the recipes with more or less liquid to accomplish your desired degree of moisture.

TWICE BAKED POTATOES ❋

PREP TIME: 15 MINUTES | COOK TIME: 60 MINUTES | READY IN: 75 MINUTES

Simple twice baked potatoes are elevated to star status with Comte or Gruyère cheese, jumbo lump crab and Greek yogurt. These make a pretty presentation and are always a hit.

MAKES 8 SERVINGS

4 whole russet potatoes

¾ cup Gruyère or Comte cheese

4 tablespoons minced chives

¾ cup Greek yogurt

5 tablespoons butter, melted

¼ teaspoon kosher salt

¼ teaspoon freshly ground black pepper

1 pound jumbo lump crabmeat

1. Preheat the oven to 325°F. Bake the potatoes for 40 minutes.

2. Cut the baked potatoes in half and remove the flesh, being careful not to break them. Reserve the potato shells. Put the potato flesh in a large bowl.

3. Add the cheese, chives, yogurt, butter, salt and pepper. Mix well, taste and adjust the seasoning.

4. Gently fold in the crabmeat. Season the reserved potato shells with salt and pepper and stuff the mixture into the shells.

5. Return the potatoes to the oven and bake them until they begin to brown.

MASHED BUTTERNUT SQUASH 🍁

PREP TIME: 10 MINUTES | COOK TIME: 20 MINUTES | READY IN: 30 MINUTES

With a few simple flavor additions, such as lime juice, curry, cinnamon, and honey, these sweet potatoes come to life as a fabulous side dish or even a stuffing for a roast pork loin.

MAKES 5 SERVINGS

1 medium (about 1 pound) butternut squash

3 tablespoons cultured butter

1 teaspoon local honey

Juice of ½ lime

¼ cup fresh local apple cider

Pinch of cinnamon

Pinch of curry powder

Kosher salt, to taste

Freshly ground black pepper, to taste

Chopped fresh chives, for garnish

1. Cut the squash in half and remove the seeds. Steam the squash halves in a stove-top steamer until fork tender, about 20 minutes.

2. Scoop out the squash flesh and put in a large bowl. Add the butter, honey, lime juice, cider, cinnamon, and curry; mash until smooth.

3. Season with salt and pepper to taste and garnish with chives before serving.

ROASTED SWEET POTATO WITH PEANUTS ✱

PREP TIME: 10 MINUTES | COOK TIME: 45 MINUTES | READY IN: 55 MINUTES

These delicious sweet potatoes are amazing with the herby and sweet compound butter. The addition of gourmet Virginia peanuts makes the recipe good as a side dish for special occasions.

MAKES 2 SERVINGS

1 medium sweet potato

4 tablespoons organic cultured butter

1 tablespoon chopped fresh thyme

½ teaspoon Vermont maple syrup

1 heaping tablespoon whole fat sour cream

Kosher salt, to taste

Freshly ground black pepper, to taste

⅓ cup crushed gourmet peanuts

1. Preheat the oven to 375°F.

2. Roast the sweet potato until fork tender, about 40 minutes.

3. Mix together the butter, thyme, maple syrup, and sour cream.

4. Slice the sweet potato open and season with salt and pepper; then add some of the butter mixture.

5. Top with the crushed peanuts.

Chef's Note: These are very interesting and delicious and a super way to introduce kids to the slightly different flavor of sweet potatoes.

BRUSSELS SPROUTS WITH MORNAY SAUCE ❦

PREP TIME: 10 MINUTES | COOK TIME: 30 MINUTES | READY IN: 40 MINUTES

A simply delicious method of preparing Brussels sprouts with a cheesy sauce that is baked to perfection. This recipe is a favorite of mine that was handed down from my Mom. It's a must-have holiday recipe at our house. Steaming Brussels sprouts on a stove top steamer is simple. Bring a pot at least half way full of water to a boil. Place the Brussels sprouts in a steamer basket in no more than two layers. With the pot covered and the basket fitting securely on the top, cook the sprouts for about ten minutes.

MAKES 10 SERVINGS

1 pound Brussels sprouts, steamed and cooled

Mornay sauce (see note on page 284), to taste

Coarse whole wheat breadcrumbs (optional)

1. Preheat the oven to 350 degrees.

2. Place the steamed Brussels sprouts in an ovenproof baking or casserole dish.

3. Spoon the Mornay sauce over the Brussels sprouts. Top with the breadcrumbs, if using, and bake for 30 minutes until it's bubbly and starting to brown a bit.

CURRIED BUTTERNUT SQUASH ⚜

PREP TIME: 30 MINUTES | READY IN: 30 MINUTES

Hard-skinned squashes are healthy, inexpensive, and fabulous for applying different ethnic flavors. This recipe shines with the addition of curry, butter, and lime juice. Substitute acorn squash if need be.

MAKES 8 SERVINGS

2 whole butternut squash

5 tablespoons cultured butter (if available)

Juice of 1 lime

3 tablespoons local apple cider

3 tablespoons minced fresh chives

Pinch of cinnamon

1 teaspoon curry powder

1 tablespoon kosher salt

½ teaspoon freshly ground black pepper

1. Cut the butternut squash in half and remove the seeds. Place them in a steamer basket over boiling water and steam them for 20 to 25 minutes or until fork tender.

2. Transfer the cooked squash to a large bowl and add the butter, lime juice, apple cider, chives, cinnamon, curry, salt, and pepper. Mash and mix well and serve.

Chef's Note: Make sure the ingredients are at room temperature so they won't cool the cooked squash.

MASHED POTATOES ✳

PREP TIME: 7 MINUTES | COOK TIME: 20 MINUTES | READY IN: 27 MINUTES

Silky smooth, rich and delicious, these mashed potatoes are sure to please. Never buy potato flakes again. Making mashed potatoes from scratch is easy to do. I prefer Idaho potatoes in this recipe. They have the right starch content to make creamy mashed potatoes.

MAKES 8 SERVINGS

3 pounds Idaho potatoes, peeled and quartered

2 cups organic whole milk

1 cup organic heavy cream

4 garlic cloves

7 tablespoons unsalted butter

4 tablespoons minced fresh chives

1 teaspoon kosher salt

1 teaspoon freshly ground black pepper

1. Steam the potatoes until they are fork tender. Set aside.

2. Place a sauce pot over medium heat and add the milk, cream, garlic, and butter. Bring the mixture to a simmer being very careful not to boil. When simmering, remove from the heat.

3. Put the steamed potatoes in the bowl of a stand mixer with the paddle attachment. Add a little of the cream mixture to the potatoes and whip the potatoes.

4. Slowly add more liquid until the desired consistency is reached. Add the chives and stir for 10 seconds; then remove the potatoes from the mixer.

5. Season with salt and pepper.

Chefs Note: Any remaining liquid can be frozen for up to 2 months and used the next time you make the dish. Also, after heating the liquid, it can be kept in the sauce pot in a 200°F oven if you're not ready to finish and serve the potatoes.

PARMESAN CRISPS WITH GOAT CHEESE MOUSSE ✳

This is a delicious and simple appetizer made with grated Parmesan cheese and fresh, herb-infused local goat cheese.

MAKES 25 SERVINGS

1 cup grated Parmesan cheese

4 ounces local goat cheese

2 tablespoons organic heavy cream

½ cup Greek yogurt

1 teaspoon herbes de Provence or Italian seasoning

1. Preheat the oven to 350°F.

2. Make the Parmesan crisps by placing a teaspoon of the cheese on a nonstick silicone mat or parchment paper that has been sprayed with cooking spray.

3. Bake for no longer than 10 minutes.

4. After baking the cheese, quickly place the melted cheese disks, while they are still warm, into ramekins, or wrap around an inverted small bowl, to form them into cups.

5. Make the mousse by combining the goat cheese, cream, yogurt and seasoning in a small bowl.

6. To serve, place a small dollop of the mousse on each Parmesan crisp.

FRENCH GREEN LENTILS ❋

PREP TIME: 10 MINUTES | COOK TIME: 35 MINUTES | READY IN: 45 MINUTES

This elegant French dish with green lentils is comprised of a perfectly poached egg, a tangy mustard vinaigrette, and a love for simple cuisine. This dish can be served with a light side salad and the French vinaigrette.

MAKES 4 SERVINGS

1 cup French green lentils

3 cups low-sodium chicken broth

1 teaspoon salt

1 teaspoon black pepper

4 medium free-range eggs

2 tablespoons white vinegar

French vinaigrette dressing (page 271)

1 small bunch fresh chives, minced

1. Combine the lentils and chicken broth in a saucepan. Season with the salt and pepper. Simmer over low heat until the lentils are soft, about 30 minutes. Drain and set aside.

2. Bring about 4 cups of salted water to a slow boil in a shallow saucepan. Season the water with a pinch of salt. Add 1 tablespoon of the white vinegar.

3. Crack one egg into a small dish or ramekin. With a big spoon, get the simmering water spinning like a tornado. Carefully drop in the egg. Be careful not to overcook the egg. The egg will be poached in 2 to 3 minutes. Remove the egg with a slotted spoon and slide it gently onto a kitchen towel to drain. Repeat this process with the remaining eggs.

4. Add some French vinaigrette to the cooked lentils in a work bowl and season them with additional salt and black pepper. Carefully stir to combine.

5. To serve, place one poached egg on top of each lentil mound. Drizzle additional French vinaigrette on top of the egg and around the plate and sprinkle the top with chives.

ORGANIC SWEET POTATOES WITH HONEY AND TANGERINE JUICE ✳

PREP TIME: 5 MINUTES | COOK TIME: 10 MINUTES | READY IN: 15 MINUTES

This is a simple preparation for sweet potatoes that makes their taste shine. A touch of local honey, tangerine juice, and butter is all this simple dish needs.

MAKES 4 SERVINGS

2 whole sweet potatoes, peeled and cubed

2 tablespoons organic unsalted butter

2 tablespoons honey

½ cup tangerine juice

Pinch of kosher salt

Pinch of freshly ground black pepper

1. Steam the potatoes until tender, about 10 minutes.

2. Place the steamed sweet potatoes in a medium bowl. Add the butter, honey, tangerine juice, salt, and pepper and mash all until smooth.

Chef's Note: These potatoes are great in a burrito with jerk chicken, black beans and good fresh goat cheese!!

POACHED BOSC PEARS ✳

This elegant poached pear recipe is simple to make, but tastes incredible. This is perfect for your next dinner party or special meal with that significant somebody in your life. For a special touch, add a pinch of sea salt to the caramel; it will bring it to the next level.

MAKES 6 SERVINGS

4 medium Bosc pears

1 cup red wine

1 bay leaf

¼ cup sugar

5 cloves

2 tablespoons walnuts

2 tablespoons caramel sauce

1. Peel the pears. Place the pears in a Dutch oven or sauce pot.

2. Add the red wine, bay leaf, sugar, and cloves and bring the mixture to a simmer over high heat. Reduce the heat to medium and simmer for 30 minutes, checking often to determine when the pears become just fork tender, but not soft.

3. Carefully remove the pears from the poaching liquid and cool them completely.

4. Continue cooking the poaching liquid until it is reduced by half.

5. Place the poached pears on serving plates and add some walnuts, some of the thickened sauce, and some caramel sauce.

SNOW PEA AND CARROT STIR-FRY ❋ ❋

PREP TIME: 5 MINUTES | COOK TIME: 2 MINUTES | READY IN: 7 MINUTES

This is a simple stir-fry featuring snow peas, carrots, and ginger. I like to make this often when snow peas are abundant in my garden or at the farmer's market. It's a vegan's dream and takes just two minutes to cook.

MAKES 4 SERVINGS

1 tablespoon toasted sesame oil

2 cups fresh snow peas

½ cup julienned carrot

1 teaspoon grated fresh ginger

2 tablespoons low-sodium soy sauce

Pinch of Harvest Eating House Seasoning (page 278)

1. Heat a wok or sauté pan over high heat.

2. Add the oil and heat; then add the snow peas and carrots. Stir-fry for 1 minute.

3. Add the ginger, soy sauce, and Harvest Eating House Seasoning and stir-fry for only 1 minute more.

Chef's Note: The stir-fry method requires the discipline to cook the food for less time than you think it needs. Crunchy vegetables are perfect.

7 | MAIN DISHES

CINNAMON-THYME CHICKEN ❋ ✿ ❋ ❋

PREP TIME: 10 MINUTES | MARINATING TIME: 30 MINUTES
COOK TIME: 35 MINUTES | READY IN: 75 MINUTES

I make many kinds of herb and spice pastes to season all types of grilled or roasted foods. This one is very good. It goes very well on chicken or pork.

MAKES 4 SERVINGS

2 tablespoons minced thyme leaves

1 tablespoon ground coriander

2 garlic cloves, minced

2 teaspoons ground cumin

1 teaspoon ground cinnamon

Pinch of kosher salt

Freshly ground black pepper, to taste

½ cup pure olive oil

5 chicken thighs

1. Preheat a charcoal or gas grill to medium heat.

2. Make a paste by combining the thyme, coriander, garlic, cumin, cinnamon, salt, pepper, and oil in a large bowl and stir until smooth.

3. Pour the paste over the chicken in the bowl and mix well. Marinate the chicken in the mixture at least 30 minutes or longer.

4. Grill the chicken thighs over medium heat until fully cooked, approximately 35 minutes.

Chef's Note: Making wet spice pastes is a great way to add the flavors of any country. Italian, Thai, Mexican, Spanish, Greek, Jamaican, Moroccan; you name it. Be creative. These wet spice pastes or rubs bring tons of flavor to the finished grilled chicken or even steak.

CHICKEN MARSALA ✳✳✳✳

PREP TIME: 10 MINUTES | COOK TIME: 25 MINUTES | READY IN: 35 MINUTES

Learn how to make this Italian favorite with organic chicken breasts and fresh mushrooms. Chicken Marsala is easy to make and delicious. I like to make this with mushrooms I find in the woods on my farm, usually they are chanterelles.

MAKES 4 SERVINGS

4 (6-ounce) free-range chicken breasts, pounded thin

1 cup all-purpose flour

5 tablespoons extra-virgin olive oil, divided

2 tablespoons minced shallots

1 tablespoon minced garlic

2 cups cremini mushrooms, sliced

Kosher salt, to taste

Pinch of freshly ground black pepper

¼ cup Marsala wine

2 tablespoons organic unsalted butter

2 tablespoons fresh thyme

1 tablespoon lemon juice

1 tablespoon minced fresh parsley

1. Dredge the chicken breasts in flour and shake off any excess.

2. Heat 2 tablespoons of the olive oil in a skillet. Panfry the chicken until browned on both sides. Remove the chicken from the skillet and set aside.

3. Add 2 tablespoons more oil to the pan. Add the shallots and thyme and cook for 1 minute.

4. Add the mushrooms, salt, and pepper. If more oil is needed, add the final tablespoon of olive oil.

5. Deglaze the pan with the Marsala wine.

6. Add the cold butter to the pan and swirl until melted. Season with salt and pepper. Remove the sauce from the heat.

7. Place the chicken on serving plates and squeeze the lemon juice on top. Add the Marsala sauce and mushrooms and garnish with parsley.

Chef's Note: To make chicken Marsala, I suggest using good Marsala wine. Chicken Marsala made with cheap wine is not very pleasing.

CHICKEN AND ASPARAGUS STIR-FRY ✳

PREP TIME: 10 MINUTES | COOK TIME: 10 MINUTES | READY IN: 20 MINUTES

Local spring asparagus adds crunch and color to this simple stir-fry dish. Be sure to use asparagus that are very fresh; look for tight ends that are not falling apart. I never make this dish after the asparagus go out of season in my area. This dish is at its best from mid-April to the end of June in most parts of the country.

MAKES 4 SERVINGS

2 teaspoons reduced-sodium soy sauce

1 teaspoon honey

2 teaspoons sesame oil

1¾ pounds asparagus, trimmed and cut on the diagonal into 1-inch pieces

1 garlic clove, minced

3 cups sliced cooked chicken breast

1 teaspoon sesame seeds (optional)

1. Combine the soy sauce and honey in a small bowl. Set aside.

2. Heat the oil in a large skillet or wok over medium-high heat. Add the asparagus and garlic. Cook for 4 minutes, stirring frequently.

3. Toss in the chicken and soy sauce mixture. Cook for about 5 minutes until heated through.

4. Sprinkle with sesame seeds, if desired.

Chef's Note: This is great served with steamed brown rice or whole wheat couscous.

TROPICAL CHICKEN QUESADILLA ✳

PREP TIME: 10 MINUTES | COOK TIME: 5 MINUTES | READY IN: 15 MINUTES

A delightful mix of chicken breast, wilted spinach, fresh goat cheese, black beans and mango salsa, this recipe never fails to impress. It is perfect as a light spring meal with a cold beer.

MAKES 4 SERVINGS

1 ounce fresh goat cheese, not aged

2 (10-inch) pieces organic lavash bread or whole wheat tortillas

2 ounces cooked chicken breast shredded or diced

¼ cup organic canned black beans, drained

1 ounce fresh spinach (a large handful)

3 tablespoons fresh cilantro

Harvest Eating House Seasoning (page 278), to taste

½ cup mango salsa (page 229)

1. Spread the goat cheese evenly on both sides of each lavash or tortilla.

2. Layer the chicken, beans, and spinach, dividing evenly between both pieces of bread or tortilla.

3. Season with the cilantro and Harvest Eating House Seasoning and fold in half to close.

4. Heat a skillet over medium low. Place the folded lavash or tortillas in the pan and cook until it starts to brown. Carefully flip and cook the second side for approximately 2 more minutes. Serve with the mango salsa.

Chef's Note: Lavash is Armenian cracker bread available in most supermarkets and Middle Eastern markets.

CHICKEN WITH WILD MUSHROOM SAUTÉ ❋

PREP TIME: 10 MINUTES | COOK TIME: 15 MINUTES | READY IN: 25 MINUTES

This recipe features meaty mushrooms that serve as a delicious bed for grilled chicken. I like to mix and match the mushrooms to keep it interesting.

MAKES 2 SERVINGS

2 boneless, skinless chicken breast halves

2 tablespoons pure olive oil

Pinch of kosher salt

Pinch of freshly ground black pepper

1 tablespoon chopped fresh oregano

1 tablespoon chopped fresh cilantro

1 tablespoon chopped fresh chives

1 tablespoon chopped fresh rosemary

¼ cup freshly squeezed lemon juice

4 tablespoons extra-virgin olive oil

1 tablespoon lemon zest

1 cup mushroom sauté (page 95)

1. Preheat a charcoal or gas grill to medium heat.

2. Brush the chicken breasts with the olive oil and season with the salt and pepper. Grill the chicken over high heat for approximately 7 minutes per side or until chicken is browned and firm to the touch.

3. While the chicken is cooking, make the "spritz" by combining the oregano, cilantro, chives, rosemary, lemon juice, 4 tablespoons of extra-virgin olive oil, and the lemon zest.

4. Serve the cooked chicken breast on top of some of the mushroom sauté and spoon some "spritz" over the top.

Chef's Note: When using a whole chicken breast, be aware that there is a little bit of cartilage that holds the breasts together. Be sure to remove it.

CHICKEN, ASPARAGUS, AND BELL PEPPER STIR FRY ✳

PREP TIME: 10 MINUTES | COOK TIME: 7 MINUTES | READY IN: 17 MINUTES

This delicious Asian stir-fry with chicken, asparagus, and peppers is easy to make. It's perfect for late spring when asparagus are still around and the first bell peppers are coming into harvest.

MAKES 4 SERVINGS

2 tablespoons pure olive oil

1 (10 to 12-ounce) organic chicken breast, chopped into 1-inch pieces

1 cup chopped fresh asparagus

1 cup chopped red bell pepper

½ cup chopped green onion

1 tablespoon minced fresh ginger

1 tablespoon toasted sesame oil

1 tablespoon low-sodium soy sauce

1 teaspoon kosher salt

½ teaspoon freshly ground black pepper

1 cup brown rice, cooked according to package directions

1. Heat a wok or nonstick pan over high heat. Add the olive oil. When the oil is hot, add the chicken and begin stir-frying. Add the asparagus, bell pepper, green onion, and ginger. Next, add the sesame oil and soy sauce; then season with the salt and pepper.

2. Move the items around in the pan. Remember, stir-frying is "noisy," with lots of sizzling. If you don't hear the noise, then you're just steaming the food. Stir-fry about 5 minutes or so, until the chicken is fully cooked.

3. Serve over the cooked brown rice.

CHICKEN PICCATA ☀ 🍁 ❄ ❋

PREP TIME: 10 MINUTES | COOK TIME: 10 MINUTES | READY IN: 20 MINUTES

Chicken Piccata is a delicate chicken recipe with a butter sauce, lemon, and capers. A dash of fresh parsley adds color and flavor. You cannot accuse this dish of being bland!

MAKES 2 SERVINGS

1 pound organic chicken breast, cut into two filets and pounded thin

Kosher salt, to taste

A few twists of freshly ground black pepper

5 teaspoons spice blend

5 tablespoons light olive oil

⅔ cup all-purpose flour

½ cup dry white wine, such as Chablis

⅔ cup organic chicken stock

3 tablespoons lemon juice

Zest of lemon

2 tablespoons capers

5 tablespoons unsalted butter

¼ cup chopped fresh parsley

1. Season the chicken breasts with the salt, pepper, and your favorite spice blend. See Chef's Note.

2. Heat the oil in a sauté pan over medium heat.

3. Pour the flour into a shallow dish or plate with edges. Dredge the chicken breasts in the flour, shaking off any excess flour. Place the flour-coated chicken in the sauté pan and cook until slightly browned. Transfer the chicken to a baking sheet and keep warm in a 170°F oven.

4. With the sauté pan still over medium, deglaze by adding the white wine and cooking until it reduces by half. Add the chicken stock, lemon juice, lemon zest, and capers.

5. Continue cooking to reduce the mixture for a few more minutes. Turn off the heat and whisk in the butter and parsley to slightly thicken the sauce. Serve the sauce over the chicken.

Chef's Note: Herbes de Provence is a good choice of spice blend for this dish.

GRILLED CHICKEN PARMESAN ☀

PREP TIME: 15 MINUTES | COOK TIME: 35 MINUTES | READY IN: 50 MINUTES

This simple dish has added flavor from the grilling process. Unlike traditional breaded Parmesan, this one is lower in fat and much easier to prepare because the breading is eliminated. It's a favorite recipe of fans of HarvestEating.com.

MAKES 6 SERVINGS

3 whole skinless, boneless chicken breasts, pounded thin

¼ cup pure olive oil

5 tablespoons Herbes de Provence)

5 cups tomato sauce

1 pound mozzarella cheese, grated

¾ cup grated Parmesan cheese

1. Toss the chicken breasts, oil, and seasoning together in a bowl. Marinate for 10 minutes. While the chicken is marinating preheat the charcoal or gas grill to medium heat.

2. Remove the chicken from the marinade, discarding the marinade. Grill the marinated chicken for about 3 minutes on one side. Turn the breasts and grill them for 2 minutes on the other side.

3. Arrange the grilled chicken in an oven-safe baking dish and cover them with the tomato sauce and grated cheeses. Bake until bubbly and starting to brown, about 10 minutes.

HARVEST CHICKEN 🍁

PREP TIME: 15 MINUTES | COOK TIME: 30 MINUTES | READY IN: 45 MINUTES

This recipe is very complex with strong flavors from olives, wine, lemon, and green onions. Try to buy your olives loose from a good specialty store and look for naturally raised chicken.

MAKES 4 SERVINGS

2 pounds skinless, boneless organic free-range chicken breasts

¼ cup Dijon mustard

1 tablespoon extra-virgin olive oil

¼ cup dry white wine

Pinch of salt

Pinch of freshly ground black pepper

½ teaspoon paprika

1 medium organic lemon

¼ cup green olives (8 to 10 large olives)

4 sprigs fresh thyme, rinsed

2 medium cooking tomatoes, chopped

2 bunches green onions, chopped (3 cups)

1. Preheat the oven to 375°F.

2. Remove any excess fat from the chicken breasts. Set aside.

3. In a small mixing bowl, whisk together the Dijon mustard, olive oil, white wine, salt, pepper, and paprika.

4. Roll the chicken breasts in the sauce and place in a baking dish. Wash the lemon and grate (or zest) the lemon peel over the chicken. Squeeze the juice from ½ the lemon over the chicken.

5. Place the green olives around the chicken. Place the thyme sprigs over the chicken and toss the chopped tomatoes and green onions over the chicken.

6. Bake for 30 minutes, or until cooked through.

7. Spoon the juices over the chicken from time to time and pour the juices over each individual piece of chicken before serving.

Chef's Note: Make sure to only grate the yellow part of the lemon peel. The white part, or pith, is quite bitter.

CHICKEN BREASTS WITH CIDER MUSTARD SAUCE ✳

PREP TIME: 10 MINUTES | COOK TIME: 20 MINUTES | READY IN: 30 MINUTES

I always serve this dish when the first local apples of the season become available. Using good unfiltered cider adds great flavor to the sauce. The tang of high-quality French Dijon mustard is the key to a great sauce. This is a very popular recipe on the Harvest Eating website.

MAKES 4 SERVINGS

⅓ cup extra-virgin olive oil

2 boneless, skinless organic chicken breasts, thinly sliced

Kosher salt, to taste

Freshly ground black pepper, to taste

All-purpose flour for dredging

1 small shallot, minced

¼ cup real apple cider, unfiltered

1 tablespoon organic heavy cream

1 tablespoon Dijon mustard

1 small garlic clove, minced (optional)

Fresh herbs for garnish (thyme, chives, or rosemary)

1. Heat the oil in a heavy-bottomed pan over medium high.

2. Season the chicken breasts with salt and pepper and dredge them in the flour. Add to the pan.

3. Cook the chicken until nicely browned on each side, about 2 minutes per side. Transfer the cooked chicken to a hot plate and cover to keep warm.

4. For the sauce: add the shallot and more oil, if necessary, to the pan. Sauté for 1 minute longer.

5. Add the cider and deglaze the pan using a whisk to scrape up any brown bits. Add the cream, mustard, and garlic, if using and stir to combine. Taste and adjust the seasonings. To thicken the sauce, cook a little longer. If it's too thick, add a little more cider.

6. Pour the sauce over the chicken and garnish with fresh herbs.

CHICKEN CURRY ✳

PREP TIME: 20 MINUTES | COOK TIME: 35 MINUTES | READY IN: 55 MINUTES

This is a delicious and healthy dish made with seasonal vegetables, coconut milk, and curry. Feel free to use hot sauce, chilies, or other spicy additions according to your tastes.

MAKES 6 SERVINGS

2 tablespoons olive oil

½ cup diced onion

½ cup diced carrot

½ cup cubed turnip (half-inch cubes)

½ cup cubed butternut squash (half-inch cubes)

½ cup cubed white potatoes (half-inch cubes)

3 tablespoons curry powder

1 cup organic chicken stock (optional)

1 (13½-ounce) can organic unsweetened coconut milk

Kosher salt, to taste

A few twists of freshly ground black pepper

Fresh cilantro, for garnish

1. Heat the oil in a heavy-bottomed pot over medium heat. Add the onion and sauté for 1 minute.

2. Add the carrot, turnip, squash, potatoes, curry powder, chicken stock, if using, salt, and pepper. Cook for a few minutes; then add the coconut milk. Reduce heat to low, cover, and cook for 25 minutes. Garnish with cilantro.

Chef's Note: Serve over white rice, garnish with cilantro, and enjoy.

HERB ROASTED TURKEY ✦

PREP TIME: 15 MINUTES | COOK TIME: 45 MINUTES | READY IN: 60 MINUTES

We often buy organic turkey breasts in the fall and make this dish. We slice thin the leftover turkey for sandwiches and for turkey salad. Good stuff for sure.

MAKES 12 SERVINGS

4 to 5 pounds naturally-raised turkey breast

2 organic celery stalks, cut into 1-inch pieces

2 organic carrots, cut into 1-inch pieces

1 large onion, diced

Kosher salt, to taste

Freshly ground black pepper, to taste

2 ounces butter, softened

1 tablespoon chopped fresh rosemary

2 tablespoons chopped fresh sage

1. Preheat the oven to 375°F.

2. Place the celery, carrots, and onion in a sturdy roasting dish and place the turkey breast on top of the vegetables.

3. Make the herb butter by combining the softened butter, rosemary, and sage. Brush the entire surface of the turkey breast with the herb butter.

4. Roast the turkey until an instant or probe thermometer reads 165°F. Remove the turkey from the oven and let it rest covered with a foil tent. The turkey will continue to cook to approximately 170°F. After the turkey is well rested, slice it and serve.

Chef's Note: This same technique can be used for a whole turkey, goose or duck.

CARIBBEAN CHICKEN ✳

PREP TIME: 10 MINUTES | COOK TIME: 45 MINUTES | READY IN: 55 MINUTES

This is a slow-braised chicken dish with sweet potatoes, green bell peppers, and coconut milk. The flavorful cilantro-scented broth becomes a rich sauce. Butternut squash can be used in place of sweet potatoes. This recipe is a winner on HarvestEating.com.

MAKES 4 SERVINGS

½ cup all-purpose flour

2 tablespoons ground cumin

2 tablespoons chopped fresh sage

Kosher salt, to taste

Freshly ground black pepper, to taste

4 chicken legs with thighs attached, skin on

4 tablespoons olive oil

1 cup diced organic green or red bell pepper

1 cup diced organic white onion

2 cups organic or homemade chicken broth

1 cup organic unsweetened coconut milk

1 large sweet potato, peeled and cut into 1-inch cubes

1 bunch fresh cilantro, chopped, reserve some for garnish

1. Combine the flour, cumin, sage, salt and pepper. Dredge the chicken in the flour.

2. Heat the oil in a Dutch oven over medium-high heat. Add the chicken and sauté it until well-browned on all sides, approximately 10 minutes.

3. Add the bell pepper and onion and season with additional salt and pepper to taste. Sauté for 5 minutes more.

4. Add the chicken broth, coconut milk, sweet potato, and cilantro. Cover and cook for 30 minutes.

5. Remove the chicken and keep warm. Thicken the sauce with a slurry made from equal parts cold water and cornstarch.

6. When thickened, pour the sauce over the chicken and garnish with additional cilantro.

Chef's Note: This dish goes well with rice and black beans and a cold beer!

ALMOND-CRUSTED CHICKEN TENDERS ✳

PREP TIME: 10 MINUTES | COOK TIME: 12 MINUTES | READY IN: 22 MINUTES

Here is a simple and healthy way to provide your kids with some great nutrition. Almonds are rich in omega-3 oil, chicken provides protein, and yogurt is a great source of calcium. Many adults find this recipe a hit as well.

MAKES 4 SERVINGS

½ cup egg whites (from about 4 large free-range eggs)

1 cup crushed almonds

2 pounds local, organic chicken tenders

2 cups pure olive oil for frying

⅛ teaspoon kosher salt

A twist of freshly ground black pepper

1 cup Greek-style yogurt

1 tablespoon Dijon mustard

2 teaspoons local honey

1. Place the egg whites in a shallow bowl or pie plate. Place the almonds in a second shallow bowl or pie plate. Dredge the chicken tenders in the egg whites then dip each one in the almonds to coat them evenly.

2. Heat 2 tablespoons of the olive oil in a non-stick skillet over medium heat. Add the chicken four pieces at a time and cook for about 5 minutes per side until cooked through and golden brown. They will be firm to the touch when cooked.

3. Season with salt and pepper. Repeat with the remaining chicken until all used. Set the chicken aside.

4. Combine the yogurt, mustard, and honey in a bowl; mix well. Serve with the chicken as a dipping sauce.

Chef's Note: Yellow mustard can be used for less sophisticated taste buds. Salt and pepper can be added to the sauce if you feel the need!

CHICKEN MUSHROOM MOUSSE ❄

PREP TIME: 15 MINUTES | COOK TIME: 10 MINUTES | READY IN: 25 MINUTES

Chicken mushroom mousse is simple to prepare. It's made from poached chicken and mushrooms and is perfect for a rustic dinner party. The liquid smoke, which is naturally derived, is optional.

MAKES 6 SERVINGS

2 tablespoons extra-virgin olive oil

2 cups chopped wild mushrooms

1 medium shallot, chopped

2 tablespoons chopped fresh thyme

½ cup dry white wine

4 (4-ounce) chicken thighs, poached and cooled

1 teaspoon liquid smoke

1 teaspoon kosher salt

½ teaspoon freshly ground black pepper

1 cup heavy cream, divided

1 medium loaf ciabatta bread, sliced and toasted

1. **To create the mushroom duxelles:** Heat the olive oil in a sauté pan over medium-low heat. Add the mushrooms and stir. Add the shallot and thyme. Sauté for 5 minutes, until the mushrooms are cooked and slightly reduced. Deglaze the pan with the white wine and scrape up any flavorful bits from the bottom of the pan. Remove from the heat.

2. Place the chicken thighs, mushroom duxelles, liquid smoke, salt, and pepper into a food processor. Process until broken down into a fine paste.

3. Add ¼ cup of the cream to the mixture and process. Drizzle more cream through the top of the processor as it mixes. Mix until it reaches a mousse-like consistency. It should be light but stand firmly on a spoon.

4. Spread the mousse onto the ciabatta bread. Garnish each slice with fresh rosemary or thyme and serve.

Chef's Note: Chicken breasts can be substituted if dark meat is not your preference. I personally would not make it with white meat.

CHICKEN POT PIE ✳

PREP TIME: 30 MINUTES | COOK TIME: 60 MINUTES | READY IN: 90 MINUTES

Learn how-to-make chicken pot pie, a comfort-food classic, with seasonal root vegetables, velouté sauce, and home-made piecrust. To poach the chicken, simmer it in water for about 10 minutes or until there is no longer any pink.

MAKES 10 SERVINGS

1 recipe Pastry Dough (page 288)

Dried beans or pie weights (for prebaking the piecrust)

2 tablespoons extra-virgin olive oil

¼ cup chopped organic white onion

¼ cup chopped organic celery

Pinch of kosher salt

Pinch of freshly ground black pepper

½ cup cubed butternut squash

½ cup cubed organic potato

½ cup cubed rutabaga or turnip

3 cups organic chicken breast, poached and cubed or shred-ded

¼ cup fresh peas

2 cups velouté sauce (page 284)

1. Preheat the oven to 350 degrees.

2. On a floured surface, roll the pastry dough into a round pie crust, approximately ¼-inch thick. Place the crust into a nonstick deep, round 10-inch pie pan. Trim the excess crust from around the rim of the pan and set aside.

3. Cover the dough in the pan with aluminum foil being sure you cover the edges of the crust. Place the dry beans or pie weights on top of the foil to weigh down the dough. Bake for 15 minutes. Remove the baked piecrust from the oven and remove the aluminum foil and beans or pie weights. Do not turn off the oven.

4. Heat the oil in a saucepan over low heat. Sauté the oil, onion, and celery enough to release their flavors, but do not brown. Season with salt and pepper.

5. Steam the butternut squash, potato, and rutabaga or turnip until tender, about 5 minutes.

6. In a bowl, gently fold together the poached chicken, sautéed vegetables, peas, and velouté sauce. Adjust the seasonings to taste.

7. Place the filling mixture into the baked piecrust. Top with extra pieces of dough. The trimmed dough pieces can be re-rolled and cut into decorative shapes.

8. Bake the pot pie for 35 to 45 minutes, or until bubbly and golden brown on top. Be careful not to dry it out by cooking it too long. Remember everything inside the pot pie was pre-cooked, so you're just heating it up and browning the crust.

CHICKEN SATAY WITH PEANUT SAUCE ✳

This peanut sauce is awesome on chicken or tofu. The sauce is easy to make, healthy and you can freeze it for use in another recipe. It's not actually satay without being cooked on skewers but this is our version of it.

MAKES 6 SERVINGS

6 boneless, skinless chicken thighs

3 tablespoons olive oil

3 tablespoons poultry seasoning

2 tablespoons sesame oil

1 tablespoon fish sauce

1 cup organic unsweetened coconut milk

½ cup pineapple juice

½ cup organic peanut butter

1 teaspoon sriracha or similar hot sauce

3 tablespoons chopped fresh cilantro

1. Preheat a charcoal or gas grill to medium-high heat.

2. Toss the chicken thighs in the olive oil and the poultry seasoning of your choice.

3. Grill the chicken until it is fully cooked and reaches an internal temperature of 165°F.

4. To make the peanut sauce, combine the sesame oil, fish sauce, coconut milk, pineapple juice, peanut butter, hot sauce, and cilantro. Mix well.

5. Serve the chicken with rice and beans or a seasonal vegetable and the peanut sauce for dipping.

TANDOORI-STYLE CHICKEN ✻

PREP TIME: 5 MINUTES | MARINATING TIME: 30 MINUTES
COOK TIME: 20 MINUTES | READY IN: 55 MINUTES

The chicken in this recipe is marinated in a tangy sauce of yogurt, buttermilk, curry powder, coriander, cilantro, and lime juice. The acidity in the yogurt and buttermilk helps tenderize the chicken. The combination of spices used makes the flavor really beautiful.

MAKES 6 SERVINGS

½ cup organic buttermilk

1 tablespoon ground coriander

1 tablespoon curry powder

½ cup plain yogurt

3 tablespoons chopped fresh cilantro, stems included

2 tablespoons freshly squeezed lime juice

Pinch of kosher salt

5 to 6 boneless, skinless (free-range) chicken thighs

1. For the marinade, combine the buttermilk, coriander, curry powder, yogurt, cilantro, lime juice and salt. Mix well.

2. Add the chicken thighs and marinate for at least 30 minutes and up to 2 hours.

3. Preheat a charcoal or gas grill to medium heat.

4. Grill the chicken until done, or the juice runs clear when pierced with a fork.

Chef's Note: A tandoor is a cylindrical clay oven used in Transcaucasia, the Balkans, the Middle East, Central Asia, Pakistan, India and Bangladesh. In it, food is cooked over a hot charcoal fire. Temperatures in a tandoor can approach 900°F and it is common for tandoor ovens to remain lit for long periods of time to maintain the high cooking temperature.

CUBAN PORK ROAST SANDWICHES ❋ ❋ ❋ ❋

PREP TIME: 15 MINUTES | COOK TIME: 4 HOURS | READY IN: 4¼ HOURS

This Cuban pork dish brings tons of flavors and is so tender. The combination of spices makes your mouth sing. It is very classic when accompanied by black beans. Use leftovers for pressed Cuban sandwiches or to make burritos.

MAKES 15 SERVINGS

2 tablespoons ground cumin

2 tablespoons garlic powder

2 tablespoons dried oregano

2 tablespoons Spanish paprika

2 tablespoons salt

2 tablespoons black pepper

Zest of 1 medium orange

Juice of ½ medium orange

1 bunch cilantro leaves, chopped

3 tablespoons olive oil

4 pounds pork shoulder

Butter for grilling

Swiss cheese, ham, and pickles
    for serving

1. Preheat the oven to 275°F. Combine the cumin, garlic powder, oregano, paprika, salt, and pepper in a bowl.

2. In a separate bowl, combine the orange zest, orange juice, cilantro, and olive oil. Add to the dry ingredients and mix well to form a wet paste.

3. Rub the paste all over the pork shoulder.

4. Place the pork in a covered Dutch oven or roasting dish with 1 cup water.

5. Roast for 3 to 4 hours or until extremely tender. Let the pork rest in the refrigerator overnight before making the sandwiches.

6. Just before serving, split the rolls, spread the inside of each roll with 1 tablespoon butter, and grill them, cut side down, over medium heat until toasted, about 30 seconds.

7. Layer each roll with Swiss cheese, ham, pickle slices, and sliced pork loin. Flatten the sandwiches on a cutting board with the palm of your hand and then grill them over direct medium heat for 30 seconds. Turn the sandwiches and press down firmly with a spatula (you can even place a cast-iron skillet on top of the sandwiches) and grill for 30 seconds more. Serve warm or at room temperature.

Chef's Note: Crumbled bacon and sliced Manzanillo Spanish olives are great on top! This is good served with rice and beans.

GRILLED PORK CHOPS WITH CONFETTI RICE ☀

PREP TIME: 10 MINUTES | COOK TIME: 25 MINUTES | READY IN: 35 MINUTES

I love grilled pork chops especially when I buy them from my friend Jamie Ager in Fairview, North Carolina. Getting good pork is becoming tougher (no pun intended), but there still is good pork to be had.

MAKES 1 SERVING

1 (6-ounce) naturally-raised pork chop

Pinch of kosher salt

Pinch of freshly ground black pepper

1 tablespoon olive oil

2 tablespoons walnut pesto

1 tablespoon orange juice

Pinch of orange zest

1½ cups water

1 cup rice

2 tablespoons minced organic carrot

2 tablespoons minced green bell peppers

2 tablespoons minced zucchini

3 tablespoons minced red onion

1 tablespoon spice blend (such as herbes de Provence, or salt, pepper and garlic)

1 tablespoon organic unsalted butter

1. Prepare a charcoal or gas grill to medium hot.

2. Season the pork chop with salt, pepper, and olive oil.

3. Place the chop on a medium-hot clean grill and cook for about 6 minutes per side until a thermometer reads 155°F internal temperature.

4. Top the grilled chop with the basil walnut pesto, orange juice and orange zest.

5. Bring the water to a boil in a pot with a lid.

6. Add the rice, carrot, bell pepper, zucchini, red onion, Herbs de Provence and butter. Cover the pot and cook over medium-low heat for 15 minutes. Let it rest off the heat covered for 2 minutes. Serve with the pork chops.

PAN-FRIED PORK CHOPS *

PREP TIME: 20 MINUTES | COOK TIME: 15 MINUTES | READY IN: 35 MINUTES

This dish is satisfying, crispy, luscious and full of great comfort food flavor. It goes well with cabbage slaw, steamed red-skinned potatoes, and a cold light beer.

MAKES 4 SERVINGS

- 1 cup all-purpose flour
- 1 free-range egg, beaten
- ½ cup plain breadcrumbs
- 1 tablespoon garlic powder
- 1 teaspoon dried thyme (optional)
- Kosher salt, to taste
- Freshly ground black pepper, to taste
- 4 center-cut, bone-in pork chops
- ¼ cup pure or extra-virgin olive oil, for frying

1. Place the flour in a shallow pan or bowl. Place the beaten egg in a second bowl and the breadcrumbs in a third bowl. Season the flour and breadcrumbs using the garlic powder, thyme, if using, salt and pepper.

2. In a three-step process, dredge each pork chop in the flour. Shake off any excess, then dredge them in the egg and then in the breadcrumbs, pressing the crumbs on the chops to completely cover them.

3. Heat the oil in a large cast-iron skillet over medium low.

4. When the oil is hot, add the chops to the pan. Slowly fry them, turning after 8 to 10 minutes. Cook 5 to 6 minutes more on the second side.

Chef's Note: Make sure the oil is not too hot, or the chops will burn on the outside and be raw on the inside. Cook them slowly. Very slowly.

SPICED APPLE PORK ROAST 🍁

PREP TIME: 30 MINUTES | COOK TIME: 2½ HOURS | READY IN: 3 HOURS

This is a nice recipe for colder fall months when local apples are still in season. You can make your own applesauce or use store bought. Serve with your favorite Harvest Eating fall vegetable recipe. Whenever possible, buy naturally raised pork.

MAKES 12 SERVINGS

1 cup applesauce

⅓ cup brown sugar (packed)

2 teaspoons vinegar

1 teaspoon Dijon mustard

⅛ teaspoon ground cloves

1 tablespoon all-purpose flour

½ teaspoon salt

¼ teaspoon sugar

⅛ teaspoon garlic powder

⅛ teaspoon freshly ground black pepper

4 pounds boneless pork roast

1. Preheat the oven to 350°F.

2. Stir together the applesauce, brown sugar, vinegar, mustard, and cloves in a small bowl; refrigerate until ready to use.

3. Combine the flour, salt, sugar, garlic powder, and pepper in another small bowl.

4. Rub flour mixture over the surface of the pork. Place the pork roast on a rack in a shallow roasting pan.

5. Roast, uncovered, until the internal temperature is 140°F. It will take about 2½ hours.

6. Spoon half of the reserved applesauce mixture over the roast and continue roasting until the internal temperature reaches 155°F, about another 30 minutes. (The rule for cooking pork is 18 to 20 minutes per pound.)

7. Transfer the roast to a serving platter; cover with foil and let stand for 15 minutes before slicing.

8. Heat the applesauce in a small saucepan over medium-high heat until boiling; boil for 1 minute. Spoon the heated applesauce mixture over the pork slices before serving.

BLACK BEAN AND CHORIZO EMPANADAS ❋

PREP TIME: 15 MINUTES | COOK TIME: 15 MINUTES | READY IN: 30 MINUTES

Empanadas are a delicious stuffed Latin-style pastry. This empanada is made with chorizo and black beans. These cook up rather quickly and have boat loads of flavor.

MAKES 10 SERVINGS

2 tablespoons pure olive oil

2 (6-inch) chorizo sausages (casings removed)

¼ cup diced organic red onion

¼ cup chopped fresh cilantro

1 (15-ounce) can organic black beans, rinsed and drained

1 package empanada wraps

Cumin, for garnish

Cumin-Cilantro Crema (page 285), for garnish

1. Heat the oil over medium heat in a sauté pan. Add the sausages and cook for 10 minutes, stirring often until it's fully cooked. If the chorizo was fully cooked in the package, reduce cooking time to 5 minutes.

2. Add the red onion, cilantro, and black beans. Cook for 2 minutes.

3. Remove from the heat and mash the mixture together forming the filling for the empanadas.

4. To each empanada wrap add a heaping tablespoon of the sausage filling (be careful not to overstuff them) and press down slightly on the filling.

5. Fold the wrap in half to make a football shape. Press around the edges of the empanada wrap with your fingers to seal it, and then use the tines of a fork to crimp the edges.

6. Cook the filled empanadas in a dry, nonstick skillet over medium heat until slightly brown and crispy. This should take a few minutes per side.

7. To serve, top each empanada with a pinch of cumin and a dollop of cilantro crema.

Chef's Note: Look for frozen empanada dough in the Latin section of the grocery store freezer. Goya is a brand that makes these.

BEEF TENDERLOIN WITH HERB CRUST ✳

PREP TIME: 15 MINUTES | COOK TIME: 20 TO 30 MINUTES | READY IN: 35 TO 45 MINUTES

Grass-fed beef is more flavorful in the spring because of the nutrients in the new grass. Check out your farmer's market for local grass-fed beef.

MAKES 8 SERVINGS

1 (3½ pound) beef tenderloin, trimmed of fat

1 tablespoon olive oil

1 tablespoon Creole seasoning

2 tablespoons Dijon mustard

1 cup freshly chopped herbs (rosemary, thyme, chives, chervil)

½ teaspoon ground black pepper

2 teaspoons chopped garlic

½ teaspoon salt

1. Preheat the oven to 400°F. Rub the tenderloin with the oil and Creole seasoning.

2. Heat a large sauté pan over high heat until very hot, about 2 minutes. Sear the meat until evenly browned on all sides, about 2 minutes per side. Remove from the heat.

3. Line a shallow baking pan with aluminum foil. Place a wire rack in the pan on the foil . Place the tenderloin on the rack. Rub the top and sides of the meat with the mustard.

4. Combine the herbs, black pepper, garlic, and salt in a small mixing bowl. Using your hands, press the herb mixture evenly over the mustard on the top and sides of the tenderloin.

5. Roast the tenderloin until an instant-read thermometer reads 125 to 145 degrees, depending on your preference for temperature, about 20 minutes for medium rare and 30 minutes for medium well.

BRAISED SHORT RIBS OF BEEF WITH POTATOES ✳

PREP TIME: 15 MINUTES | COOK TIME: 3½ HOURS | READY IN: 3 HOURS 45 MINUTES

Luscious beef short ribs with potatoes make a great winter dish. It's a good way to use up your fall potatoes, and the long, slow cooking will keep your kitchen warm.

MAKES 4 SERVINGS

8 pieces bone-in beef short ribs

½ teaspoon salt

½ teaspoon ground black pepper

1 tablespoon olive oil

1 onion, roughly chopped

1 small carrot, roughly chopped

1 tablespoon whole wheat flour

1 (14.5-ounce) can low-sodium beef broth

1 tablespoon tomato paste

½ teaspoon dried thyme

1 bay leaf

2 large potatoes

1. Preheat the oven to 325°F.

2. Season the beef with the salt and pepper. Heat the oil in a large ovenproof pot over medium-high heat. Working in two batches, add the beef and cook until browned on all sides, turning often, 6 to 8 minutes. Remove to a plate.

3. Reduce the heat to medium low and add the onion and carrot. Cover and cook for 3 minutes, stirring occasionally. Stir in the flour and cook, stirring almost continuously, for 1 minute.

4. Gradually stir in the broth to make a smooth sauce. Add the tomato paste, thyme, and bay leaf. Return the beef, along with any juices on the plate, to the pot. Bring to a simmer.

5. Cover and bake until almost tender, 2 to 3 hours. Stir in the potatoes, cover, and cook until both the potatoes and the beef are tender, 20 to 30 minutes.

6. Transfer the beef and potatoes to a platter. Skim the fat from the surface of the liquid. Discard the bay leaf. Return the beef and potatoes to the pan and serve.

FLANK STEAK TACO ☀

PREP TIME: 25 MINUTES | MARINATING TIME: I HOUR | COOK TIME: 20 MINUTES
READY IN: I ¾ HOURS

The corn relish is perfect for using abundant summer corn and zucchini. It has great taste, texture and pizzazz.

MAKES 6 SERVINGS

1 large flank steak (or London broil)

Juice of 2 medium limes

½ cup chopped fresh cilantro, plus some for garnish

2 tablespoons garlic pepper

¼ cup extra-virgin olive oil

2 ears sweet corn, roasted

¼ cup pure olive oil

¼ cup chopped organic white onion

½ cup chopped zucchini

2 garlic cloves, diced

1 teaspoon diced jalapeño pepper

Kosher salt, to taste

A few twists of freshly ground black pepper

½ cup chopped fresh tomato

2 medium poblano peppers, roasted, peeled, de-seeded, and chopped

6 (6-inch) corn tortillas

Crème frâiche or sour cream

1. Put the flank steak in a large bowl. Add the lime juice, cilantro, garlic pepper, and extra-virgin olive oil. Flip the steak to coat both sides in the marinade.

2. Cover the bowl with plastic wrap and allow to marinate for at least 1 hour in the refrigerator.

3. Prepare the grill and grill the steak for 8 to 10 minutes on each side, until medium-rare. Let the steak rest.

4. While the steak rests, make the corn relish. Cut the corn off of the roasted cobs with a knife.

5. Heat the pure olive oil in a skillet. When the oil is hot, add the onion, zucchini, garlic, and jalapeño pepper. Season with the salt and black pepper. Stir and cook for a few minutes.

6. Add the fresh tomato and stir. Finally, add the corn. Re-season with a pinch of the salt and pepper. Total cook time should be 8 to 10 minutes.

7. Remove the corn relish from the heat and place in a bowl. Stir in the chopped poblano peppers.

8. After the steak has rested, slice it into thin slices against the grain. Then cut it into bite-sized chunks.

9. Fill the taco shells (tortillas) with some steak, the corn relish, and a dollop of crème fraîche and a pinch of cilantro.

Chef's Note: To roast corn and poblano peppers, toss in oil, season with salt and pepper and roast at 375°F until slightly golden brown.

MEXICAN-STYLE POT ROAST ✳

PREP TIME: 15 MINUTES | COOK TIME: 3 HOURS | READY IN: 3 ¼ HOURS

This recipe is a sure hit. The preparation takes time, but the time investment pays off handsomely later. The cumin, smoky chipotle peppers, and cloves make your taste buds very happy. This has converted many viewers into fans of Harvest Eating.

MAKES 4 SERVINGS

¼ cup bacon fat or vegetable oil

1 organic white onion, diced

1 tablespoon cumin seeds

4 whole cloves

1 chipotle pepper, chopped

¼ cup tomato paste

6 cups beef broth

3 pounds beef chuck roast

1 teaspoon kosher salt

1 teaspoon freshly ground black pepper

1 bunch cilantro, chopped

1. Heat the bacon fat or oil in a large pot over medium heat. Add the onion and cook for 5 minutes.

2. Add the cumin seeds, cloves, chipotle pepper, and tomato paste. Cook for 2 minutes. Add the beef broth and the beef.

3. Cover tightly and reduce the heat to low. Cook for 3 hours.

4. Season with the salt and pepper and add the chopped cilantro before serving.

Chef's Note: Thicken the sauce with the addition of a slurry: 5 tablespoons corn starch mixed with 5 tablespoons water. When boiled, it will thicken. Serve with rice or potatoes. Carrots and celery are optional.

BEEF BOURGUIGNON ✳

PREP TIME: 45 MINUTES | COOK TIME: 2 HOURS | READY IN: 2¾ HOURS

This classic French dish is a simple-to-make, one-pot meal. Flavorful ingredients take this simple dish to new heights. Burgundy wine, thyme, onions, and hours of marinating time infuse the meat with a lot of wine flavor.

MAKES 10 SERVINGS

3 pounds beef rump roast, cut on the bias into large cubes

1 tablespoon bacon fat

3 garlic cloves

2 bunches fresh thyme sprigs

4 cups Pinot Noir wine

1 pound button mushrooms

2 cups pearl onions

3 cups low-sodium beef broth or stock

Kosher salt, to taste

Freshly ground black pepper, to taste

¼ cup flat-leaf Italian parsley, for garnish

1. Place the beef cubes into a heavy pot or Dutch oven.

2. Place the bacon fat in a saucepan over low heat. Add the garlic and thyme and stir them into the bacon fat to create an infusion of the flavors. Turn off the heat. Pour about ½ cup of the Pinot Noir into the pan to cool down the ingredients.

3. Pour the infusion mixture over the top of the beef in its pot. If needed, add more wine until the beef is three-quarters submerged. Cover and refrigerate overnight.

4. Place the beef on the stove over medium low-heat. Add the mushrooms and onions. Add enough beef stock to make the mixture three-quarters submerged. Season the mixture liberally with the salt and pepper. Cover the pot with a tight lid and cook on low heat for 3 hours.

5. Make a slurry (equal parts corn starch and cold water) to use to thicken the stew. Add the slurry a few tablespoons at a time, stirring until it reaches the desired thickness.

6. Serve the beef with mashed potatoes. Cover the potatoes with a scoop of the stew mixture and garnish with the fresh parsley.

STANDING PRIME RIB ROAST ✳

PREP TIME: 5 MINUTES | COOK TIME: 1½ HOURS | READY IN: 1¾ HOURS

Standing rib roast is the most popular meat dish on HarvestEating.com and is certainly a perennial Christmastime favorite. Juicy prime rib roast served with traditional side dishes is a show stopper. The standing rib roast is served bone-in and carved tableside.

MAKES 10 SERVINGS

1 (8-pound) standing rib roast

3 tablespoons olive oil

1 bunch fresh rosemary
(4 tablespoons chopped)

Pinch of kosher salt

Pinch freshly ground black
pepper

3 tablespoons minced shallot

2 cups organic or homemade
beef broth

3 tablespoons cornstarch

3 tablespoons water

1. Preheat the oven to 350°F. If refrigerated, bring the roast to room temperature.

2. Rub the surface of the roast with the olive oil, rosemary, salt and pepper and place in a roaster uncovered.

3. Roast until a meat thermometer inserted in the roast shows an internal temperature of 135°F.

4. Remove the roast and let it rest while making a sauce.

5. Place roasting pan over medium-high heat; then add the shallot to the pan drippings; sauté for 1 minute. Add the beef broth and bring it to a boil.

6. Combine the cornstarch and water and whisk until well mixed. Whisk in the cornstarch slurry to thicken the sauce.

Chef's Note: The internal temperature of the roast is the best measurement. Use an oven-safe probe thermometer or instant meat thermometer.

ALMOND-COATED HALIBUT ✺ ✳

PREP TIME: 2 MINUTES | COOK TIME: 15 MINUTES | READY IN: 17 MINUTES

This simple almond coating is easy to make and goes really nicely on Halibut, which is in season and available for eight months out of the year starting in March. Substitute pine nuts for the almonds in this dish as an alternative.

MAKES 4 SERVINGS

½ cup sliced almonds

¼ cup panko breadcrumbs

1 tablespoon chopped fresh parsley

1 tablespoon butter, at room temperature

2 teaspoons fresh lemon juice

Kosher salt, to taste

Freshly ground black pepper, to taste

4 (4 to 6-ounce) fresh "wild caught" halibut fillets

1. Put the almonds, breadcrumbs, and parsley into the bowl of a food processor. Process until finely ground. With the food processor running, add the butter and lemon juice and thoroughly blend. Season with salt and pepper. Transfer to a small bowl.

2. Preheat the oven to 350°F. Grease a baking sheet with additional butter to keep the fish from sticking.

3. Arrange the halibut fillets on the baking sheet. Lightly season with salt and pepper. Gently press an equal amount of almond mixture on top of each fillet.

4. Bake the fish until cooked through, about 15 minutes, depending on the thickness of the fillets.

Chef's Note: Japanese panko breadcrumbs are coarser than regular breadcrumbs and create a deliciously crunchy crust. They can be found in most large supermarkets or in Asian markets.

PAN-ROASTED SALMON ✳

PREP TIME: 7 MINUTES | COOK TIME: 10 MINUTES | READY IN: 17 MINUTES

This salmon dish is easy to make and brings loads of flavor. The spice crust pairs well with the zing of the citrus. It can be made with other citrus juice such as lemon, lime or tangerine.

MAKES 2 SERVINGS

2 wild salmon fillets, 6 ounces each

Pinch of salt

Pinch of black pepper

2 tablespoons coriander

3 tablespoons extra-virgin olive oil

½ cup dry white wine (Chablis)

Zest of 1 whole orange

½ cup fresh-squeezed orange juice

2 tablespoons cultured butter (if available)

1. Season the salmon fillet with salt and pepper then rub in the coriander to form a crust.

2. Add the olive oil to a skillet over medium-high heat. Lay the fish flesh side down in the hot olive oil. Reduce the heat to medium low.

3. Cook slowly without moving the fillet for 4 to 5 minutes before gently flipping so as not to break the fillet.

4. Once cooked to medium (or more well done if you prefer) remove the fish and deglaze the pan with the wine. (Be sure to remove the pan from the flame before adding the wine.) Scrape the pan with a wooden spatula to remove any bits of fish and cook the wine over medium-high heat until reduced by half.

5. Once the wine is reduced by half (the pan will be almost dry), add the orange zest and juice. Scrape the bottom of the pan with a wooden spatula to break up any brown bits on the pan.

6. Turn off the heat and add the butter. Give the pan a swirl to combine the butter. Taste the sauce and adjust the seasonings as necessary.

7. Pour the sauce over the fish and serve.

Chefs Note: Coriander powder can be bought in bulk in natural food stores, or buy the seeds and grind yourself in a mortar with pestle or clean coffee grinder. Ground coriander will stay fresh for two to three months.

SEARED SALMON WITH YOGURT DILL SAUCE ❋❋❋❋

PREP TIME: 5 MINUTES | COOK TIME: 7 TO 10 MINUTES | READY IN: 15 TO 17 MINUTES

Salmon goes well with the herb dill. This simple pan-searing technique develops a nice brown crust. The yogurt dill sauce is easy and delicious and makes the perfect condiment for this salmon dish.

MAKES 2 SERVINGS

2 tablespoons pure olive oil

2 wild salmon fillets, 6 ounces each

Pinch of salt

Pinch of black pepper

1 cup plain yogurt

2 tablespoons minced fresh dill

1 tablespoon fresh lemon juice

1. Heat the oil in a cast-iron skillet over medium heat until just before it smokes.

2. Season the salmon fillets with salt and pepper then lay flesh side down in the pan.

3. Cook for 3 to 4 minutes on one side; then flip the fillets and cook an additional 2 minutes. Transfer the salmon to an ovenproof plate and place in a 175°F-oven to keep warm.

4. For the sauce: Combine the yogurt with the dill and lemon juice in a bowl. Whisk together to mix well.

5. Serve the fish with 1 to 2 tablespoons of the sauce.

Chefs Note: Any firm-fleshed fish, such as halibut, mahi mahi, or grouper, can be used.

OLIVE CAPER HALIBUT ✳ ❦

PREP TIME: 10 MINUTES | COOK TIME: 10 MINUTES | READY IN: 20 MINUTES

This is a pretty aggressive flavor and only for olive lovers. The flavors of great olives marry well with the halibut. This dish screams for a nice Portuguese red wine.

MAKES 4 SERVINGS

¼ cup green olives

¼ cup capers

1 teaspoon minced fresh ginger

⅓ cup orange juice

2 tablespoons olive oil

4 (6-ounce) fresh halibut fillets

1. Preheat the oven to 375°F.

2. Combine the olives, capers, ginger, and orange juice in a food processor and process to chop the mixture into a chunky paste.

3. Add the olive oil to an ovenproof pan or casserole dish. Place the halibut fillets in the pan. Evenly pack the olive and caper paste on top of the fillet, about ¼ inch thick.

4. Cook the fish for 8 to 10 minutes, until the flesh springs back when touched. Serve with a drizzle of extra-virgin olive oil.

EGGS WITH SALMON AND LEEKS ✳

PREP TIME: 5 MINUTES | COOK TIME: 10 MINUTES | READY IN: 15 MINUTES

This is a luxurious breakfast of fresh salmon, leeks, and eggs. Be sure to find local farm-fresh eggs. I always maintain at least three different sources for local eggs. Store-bought eggs are a real bummer in my mind.

MAKES 2 SERVINGS

½ cup chopped leeks

½ tablespoon unsalted butter

1 tablespoon clarified butter (see note on page 31)

1 medium wild-caught salmon fillet (12 ounces)

Kosher salt, to taste

A few twists of freshly ground black pepper

4 medium free-range eggs

1½ teaspoons chopped fresh dill weed

1 tablespoon crème fraîche, for garnish

1. Sauté the leeks in the unsalted butter in a small sauté pan over medium heat until soft.

2. Place a nonstick skillet over high heat and add the clarified butter. Add the salmon to the butter. Season it with salt and pepper.

3. Cook the salmon until medium. It will start to firm up and get a golden crust.

4. While the salmon is cooking, whisk the eggs in a small bowl. Season them with additional salt and pepper.

5. Remove the cooked salmon from the pan. Add the sautéed leeks and the eggs to the pan and cook, stirring to scramble the eggs.

6. Break the salmon into pieces and add it to the eggs and leeks. Keep moving the mixture around to cook it evenly.

7. Add the fresh dill.

8. When the eggs are properly cooked, fluffy and still moist, serve each with a garnish of crème fraîche and additional dill.

SOY-MARINATED SESAME-CRUSTED HALIBUT ✳

PREP TIME: 15 MINUTES | COOK TIME: 15 MINUTES | READY IN: 30 MINUTES

This is a delicious soy-marinated, sesame-crusted halibut fillet with snow pea and ginger stir-fry. Healthy, light, and super easy to make. It's a very popular recipe on HarvestEating.com.

MAKES 2 SERVINGS

1 (12-ounce) Pacific halibut fillet

½ cup soy sauce

½ cup all-purpose flour

2 tablespoons black sesame seeds

2 tablespoons white sesame seeds

1½ tablespoons butter or olive oil

2 tablespoons sesame ginger vinaigrette (page 226)

SNOW PEA CARROT SAUTÉ

1 tablespoon clarified butter or canola oil

1 tablespoon minced fresh ginger

½ carrot, julienned

½ cup snow peas

Kosher salt, to taste

Freshly ground black pepper, to taste

1. Preheat the oven to 375°F.

2. Marinate the fillet in the soy sauce for about 10 minutes. Marinating longer will produce salty fish.

3. Remove the fillet from the soy sauce. Combine the flour and sesame seeds in a shallow bowl and dredge the fillet in the mixture.

4. Heat the butter or oil in an ovenproof skillet over medium heat. Add the encrusted fillet.

5. Cook for about 2 minutes, then turn the fish and place the skillet in the oven for about 5 minutes.

6. Make the snow pea carrot sauté: Heat a stainless steel skillet or a wok over high heat. Add the butter or oil, then add the ginger and cook for 30 seconds.

7. Add the carrots and cook for 1 minute. Then add the snow peas.

8. Cook the vegetables for another minute and season with the salt and pepper.

9. To serve, place a portion of the snow pea carrot sauté on each plate, top with the fish and drizzle the sesame vinaigrette over the top of the fish.

SEARED HALIBUT WITH MANGO COULIS ☀

PREP TIME: 10 MINUTES | COOK TIME: 12 MINUTES | READY IN: 22 MINUTES

Fresh halibut is seared then topped with a island-inspired sauce of mangos and ginger and cilantro.

MAKES 4 SERVINGS

4 (6-ounce) fresh halibut fillets

2 tablespoons olive oil

1 tablespoon Harvest Eating House Seasoning (page 278)

¼ cup all-purpose flour

1 cup diced ripe mango

1½ tablespoons chopped fresh cilantro

1 teaspoon grated fresh ginger

Pinch of kosher salt

Pinch of freshly ground black pepper

1 tablespoon freshly squeezed lime juice

⅛ cup freshly squeezed orange juice

1. Preheat the oven to 250°F.

2. Season the fish with seasoning mix and lightly dredge in the flour. Heat an ovenproof stainless steel skillet over medium-high heat. Add the olive oil.

3. Sear the fish for 4 to 5 minutes on one side, then 2 minutes on the other side. Remove from the heat and place in the oven to keep warm.

4. To make the coulis, place the mango, cilantro, ginger, salt, pepper and the lime and orange juices in a small food processor and process until smooth.

5. Serve the mango coulis on top of each fish fillet.

CLAMS WITH LINGUINE AND FRESH TOMATO SAUCE ☀

PREP TIME: 10 MINUTES | COOK TIME: 16 MINUTES | READY IN: 26 MINUTES

This dish is awesome in mid summer when tomatoes are at their best. Each year on Cape Cod, when we vacation in July, we dig fresh littleneck clams for this dish. It tastes amazing. I often add a few red pepper flakes to bring some heat to the dish.

MAKES 6 SERVINGS

1 tablespoon olive oil

1 organic white onion, chopped

2 garlic cloves, chopped

4 tomatoes, chopped

2 teaspoons chopped fresh basil

2 tablespoons chopped fresh parsley, divided

1 tablespoon chopped fresh oregano

Kosher salt, to taste

Freshly ground black pepper, to taste

1 cup organic chicken broth

24 littleneck clams

8 ounces linguine, cooked

1. Heat the oil in a nonstick skillet over medium. When the oil is hot, add the onion and garlic and cook for about 2 minutes.

2. Add the tomatoes, basil, 1 tablespoon of the parsley, the oregano, salt, and pepper. Cook for 3 to 4 minutes.

3. Stir in the chicken broth and bring to a boil over high heat. Add the clams.

4. Reduce heat to medium low. Cover and gently simmer until the clams open, 5 to 10 minutes.

5. Serve the clam sauce over the cooked linguini.

CEVICHE ☀

PREP TIME: 25 MINUTES | MARINATING TIME: 2 HOURS | COOK TIME: 5 MINUTES
READY IN: 2½ HOURS

A bounty from the sea, this classic Spanish-style seafood dish is popular throughout Latin countries and uses citrus juice to pickle the fish. It also combines other great flavors like avocado and tomato.

MAKES 4 SERVINGS

8 ounces fresh bay scallops, poached and diced

8 wild caught shrimp, peeled, deveined, poached and diced

2 ounces fresh fish fillets, poached and diced

1½ cups freshly squeezed lime juice

2 tablespoons freshly squeezed lemon juice

1 tablespoon minced shallot

2 tablespoons minced jalapeño pepper

1 tablespoon hot sauce

4 tablespoons minced fresh cilantro

1 tablespoon lemon zest

1 tablespoon lime zest

Kosher salt, to taste

Freshly ground black pepper, to taste

½ cup diced avocado

½ cup diced tomato

1. Place the scallops, shrimp, and fish in a nonreactive bowl. Add the lime and lemon juices, shallot, jalapeño, hot sauce, cilantro and lemon and lime zest.

2. Chill for 2 to 3 hours.

3. Season with the salt and pepper. Add the tomato and avocado.

4. Place in serving bowls and serve with tortilla chips.

Chef's Note: I can't emphasize enough that quality seafood must be used. Using farmed fish such as tilapia or precooked pond-raised shrimp is not advised. Source the fish from a qualified fish monger and tell him or her you plan to make ceviche.

CILANTRO LIME GRILLED SHRIMP WITH COCONUT FIRE SAUCE ☀

PREP TIME: 10 MINUTES | COOK TIME: 7 MINUTES | READY IN: 17 MINUTES

This recipe has it all: great flavor, great texture, the smoky heat of chipotle peppers, and the zing of fresh lime juice. The coconut milk wraps it all in silky-smooth tropical luxury. I won the 2008 National Restaurant Association's Hot Chef Challenge Contest with a variation of this recipe.

MAKES 4 SERVINGS

1 tablespoon extra-virgin olive oil

1 (14-ounce) can organic black beans, rinsed and drained

1 garlic clove, minced

1 teaspoon kosher salt

1 teaspoon freshly ground black pepper

1 pound wild-caught jumbo shrimp, peeled, deveined, and butterflied

1 cup freshly squeezed lime juice, divided (from about 3 limes)

3 tablespoons fresh cilantro, chopped and divided

½ cup organic coconut milk

½ to 1 medium chipotle pepper, minced

1. Heat the olive oil in a saucepan over medium-high heat. Add the beans and garlic and sauté them until the beans are soft. Then mash the beans and season them with the salt and pepper. Set aside.

2. In a work bowl, add the juice of two of the limes to the shrimp. Add 2 tablespoons of the chopped cilantro. Season liberally with additional salt and black pepper. Toss the shrimp until they are evenly coated. The shrimp can marinate (covered), up to an hour or more.

3. Preheat a charcoal or gas grill to medium high.

4. Grill the shrimp over medium-high heat, butterfly-side down. The shrimp will cook in 3 to 5 minutes; turn them only once.

5. While the shrimp are grilling, begin the fire sauce. Add the remaining cilantro (about 1 tablespoon, reserving a little for garnish) and the remaining lime juice to the coconut milk. Season with salt and black pepper. Add the chipotle pepper. One whole pepper will make the sauce very hot; use ½ or ¼ of the pepper for a milder sauce. Stir well to combine.

6. Serve the shrimp on a plate with the mashed black beans and cover with the coconut fire sauce and a squeeze of lime. Garnish with lime and cilantro.

SESAME-SEARED TUNA WITH WASABI VINAIGRETTE ☀

PREP TIME: 10 MINUTES | COOK TIME: 10 MINUTES | READY IN: 20 MINUTES

Here is a light and flavorful salad made with ahi tuna, organic field greens and wasabi vinaigrette. If you like sushi, you'll love this dish.

MAKES 2 SERVINGS

1 sushi grade ahi tuna fillet
   (6 ounces), chilled

2 tablespoons black sesame
   seeds

2 tablespoons white sesame
   seeds

3 tablespoons pure olive oil

1½ cups organic field greens

½ cup julienned red bell pepper

¼ cup wasabi vinaigrette
   (page 286)

½ cup fried won ton skins

1. Coat the tuna with the sesame seeds. Heat the olive oil in a skillet over medium-high heat; then sear the tuna on all sides. Cool.

2. Combine the field greens, bell pepper, and wasabi vinaigrette and toss well. Arrange on two chilled plates.

3. Slice the tuna ½ inch thick and place on top of the salad greens.

4. Top each salad with the fried won ton skins.

....

Chef's Notes: I encourage the purchase of very high quality ahi tuna for this recipe. Also, keeping tuna cold before cooking will ensure freshness and prevent the tuna from being over-cooked.

....

SAUTÉED SHRIMP WITH MARGARITA SAUCE ☀

PREP TIME: 10 MINUTES | COOK TIME: 25 MINUTES | READY IN: 35 MINUTES

Learn how to create a delicious sautéed shrimp dish with a coconut Margarita sauce. Served with local plantation rice and organic black beans.

MAKES 2 SERVINGS

½ cup uncooked rice

1 tablespoon red bell pepper or zucchini or tomato, diced

2 tablespoons pure olive oil

2 tablespoons shallots, minced

1 garlic clove, minced

5 local, wild-caught shrimp, peeled and de-veined

3 tablespoons freshly squeezed lime juice

3 tablespoons triple sec and tequila (50-50 ratio)

¼ cup organic black beans

¼ cup organic coconut milk

3 tablespoons chopped fresh cilantro

Kosher salt, to taste

Freshly ground black pepper, to taste

1. Cook the rice according to the package instructions, adding 1 tablespoon red bell pepper or other vegetable.

2. When the rice is done, tightly pack it into two 4-ounce ramekins. Turn out the molded rice onto two serving plates.

3. Heat the oil in a skillet over high heat. Add the shallots and garlic and sauté them for 1 minute.

4. Add the shrimp and sauté them for 3 minutes. Add the lime juice and cook for another minute. Remove the pan from the heat and deglaze the pan with the liquors. Return the pan to the heat and add the beans, coconut milk, and cilantro. Season with salt and pepper.

5. Cook for a minute or two longer to reduce the pan sauce; then serve.

RATATOUILLE ☀

PREP TIME: 15 MINUTES | COOK TIME: 35 MINUTES | READY IN: 50 MINUTES

Ratatouille is not just a great movie, it's a fabulous French recipe made with abundant seasonal vegetables that grow in the Provence region which is near the Mediterranean Sea. Ratatouille is a vegetable stew of sorts, thick, rustic and delicious. I grow the ingredients each year on my farm, so making it only requires a short walk to the garden and some time.

MAKES 10 SERVINGS

5 tablespoons extra-virgin olive oil

½ cup diced white onion

2 garlic cloves, minced

3 cups diced zucchini

2 cups diced tomatoes

1 cup diced eggplant

1 cup diced summer squash

½ cup diced red bell pepper

1 tablespoon minced fresh rosemary

1 tablespoon minced fresh thyme

1 tablespoon kosher salt

¼ teaspoon freshly ground black pepper

¼ cup julienned fresh basil

1. Heat a large heavy Dutch oven or pot over medium heat. Add the oil, onion and garlic and cook for 5 minutes.

2. Add the zucchini, tomatoes, eggplant, squash, pepper, rosemary, thyme, salt and pepper. Turn the heat to low and cook, covered, for 20 minutes. Remove the lid and cook the mixture uncovered until it's nice and thick, about 5 more minutes.

3. Add the basil chiffonade, mix well and serve.

Chef's Note: This dish is a perfect demonstration of what Harvest Eating is. Using abundant seasonal vegetables to create delicious meals out of necessity. This dish was surely created as a way to use the abundance of vegetables that grow in the south of France during warmer months. Play around with the recipe, make it work for you and make it with fresh ingredients.

MACARONI AND CHEESE ❋✦❋❋

PREP TIME: 25 MINUTES | COOK TIME: 35 MINIUTES | READY IN: 60 MINUTES

"Death to boxed mac and cheese," I say. Making your own is a snap, and the full flavors from good cheese make it a great side dish. Using whole wheat pasta adds nutrition as well.

MAKES 12 SERVINGS

4 tablespoons unsalted butter

¼ cup all-purpose flour

2 cups organic whole milk

½ small white onion, diced

½ cup English farmhouse cheddar

1 cup shredded Gruyère cheese

½ pound whole wheat macaroni, cooked according to package directions

¼ teaspoon ground cloves

1 tablespoon kosher salt

1 teaspoon freshly ground black pepper

1 cup whole wheat breadcrumbs

1. Preheat the oven to 350°F.

2. In a sauce pot combine the butter and flour. Cook for 3 to 4 minutes over low heat.

3. Add the milk and onion, stirring constantly. Cook until the mixture starts to boil; then turn the heat to low.

4. The sauce should start to thicken up quickly. At this point slowly whisk in the cheeses until melted. After sauce is done, remove the onion.

5. Combine the cooked pasta in a bowl with the sauce, cloves, salt, and pepper. Mix well.

6. Place the mixture in a large casserole dish. Top it with the breadcrumbs and bake for 35 to 40 minutes.

LINGUINI WITH CLAMS ✳

Fresh clams are available year-round. Use my Homemade Pasta (page 273) to really experience an authentic Italian dish.

MAKES 6 SERVINGS

1 pound linguini

¼ cup extra-virgin olive oil, divided

3 tablespoons chopped garlic

1 cup minced shallots

1 teaspoon crushed red pepper flakes

4 pounds fresh littleneck clams

1 cup white wine

4 cups clam juice

¼ cup chopped fresh parsley

1 tablespoon salt

1. Cook the linguini for 7 to 8 minutes, and then drain. The pasta should not be cooked completely; it will finish cooking in the sauce.

2. Heat 2 tablespoons of the oil in a large skillet over medium heat.

3. Add the garlic and cook for 5 minutes or until just starting to turn color. Add the shallots and crushed red pepper flakes; continue to cook for about 5 more minutes.

4. Add the clams and wine and cook for 3 minutes to reduce the wine by half.

5. Add the clam juice and bring to a boil over high heat.

6. Add the pasta and cook covered for about 5 minutes. Add the parsley and remaining olive oil.

7. Season with salt.

PASTA PRIMAVERA ✳

PREP TIME: 15 MINUTES | COOK TIME: 25 MINUTES | READY IN: 40 MINUTES

Pasta primavera is a popular springtime dish in Italy. You can always substitute whatever vegetable is ripe in your own garden or in season at your local farmer's market.

MAKES 6 SERVINGS

1 pound penne rigate

¼ cup extra-virgin olive oil

1 small organic red onion, julienned

2 tablespoons chopped garlic

2 yellow squash, julienned

2 organic carrots, julienned

2 bell peppers (1 red and 1 green), julienned

½ pound fresh spring asparagus, cut in ½-inch pieces

1½ cups chicken broth

½ cup freshly grated parmesan cheese

⅓ cup chopped fresh basil

1. Cook the penne for about 7 to 8 minutes, and then drain. The pasta should not be cooked completely; it will finish cooking in the sauce.

2. Heat the oil in a large pan over medium heat. Add the onion and garlic and cook for about 3 minutes or until tender.

3. Add the squash, carrots, peppers, and asparagus. Cook until the vegetables become soft to the bite with some crunch, about 10 minutes.

4. Add the chicken broth and bring to a boil over high heat. Add the pasta and cover. Reduce the heat to medium and simmer for a few minutes.

5. Turn off the heat and add the cheese and basil. Stir and serve.

WHOLE WHEAT PENNE WITH SPRING PEAS & RICOTTA ✳

PREP TIME: 10 MINUTES | COOK TIME: 20 MINUTES | READY IN: 30 MINUTES

This is one of my favorite pasta recipes. I prefer to only use fresh peas, whole milk ricotta, and good pesto. Be sure to serve pasta that is al dente, which means slightly firm which is how it would be served in Italy.

MAKES 4 SERVINGS

4 ounces (1 cup) fresh spring peas

8 ounces whole wheat penne pasta

3 tablespoons basil pesto (page 232)

1 tablespoon extra-virgin olive oil

1 garlic clove, sliced

1 small shallot, sliced

8 ounces (1 cup) whole milk ricotta cheese

Parmigiano-Reggiano cheese, to taste

Kosher salt, to taste

Freshly ground black pepper, to taste

1. Steam the fresh peas until tender, about 25 minutes. (If using frozen peas, they don't take as long to cook as fresh, about 2 minutes, because they are precooked before freezing.)

2. In a large pot, bring 5 quarts of water to a boil. Add the pasta and a few tablespoons of salt. Cook the pasta until al dente, or still a little firm, about 9 minutes.

3. Heat the olive oil in a large saucepan over medium. Add the garlic and shallot and cook for 1 minute. Add the cooked peas, ricotta, pasta, and pesto.

4. Mix the ingredients well. Grate the Parmigiano-Reggiano on top and season with salt and pepper.

PAPPARADELLE WITH SPRING PEAS AND WILD MUSHROOMS ☀

PREP TIME: 10 MINUTES | COOK TIME: 25 MINUTES | READY IN: 35 MINUTES

This seasonal homemade pasta dish with spring peas, wild mushrooms and ricotta cheese is the perfect dish for spring. The whole wheat pasta retains it texture to produce a very al dente, fresh pasta dish.

MAKES 10 SERVINGS

½ pound fresh whole wheat pappardelle pasta

4 tablespoons extra-virgin olive oil

1 cup sliced wild mushrooms

1 garlic clove, minced

2 tablespoons minced shallots

1½ cups whole-milk ricotta cheese

½ cup fresh peas, precooked

Kosher salt, to taste

Freshly ground black pepper, to taste

1 tablespoon chopped fresh thyme leaves

1 tablespoon chopped fresh chives

½ cup grated Parmigiano-Reggiano cheese, plus some for serving

1. Cook the pasta in boiling water until al dente, which means slightly firm. This may take slightly longer than 3 minutes, even for fresh pasta.

2. Heat the oil in a large skillet over medium heat. Add the mushrooms and cook them for 3 to 4 minutes. Add the garlic and shallots and cook for 2 more minutes; then add the ricotta cheese and peas.

3. Continue stirring until the cheese melts. Add the cooked pasta, salt, and pepper and mix until well combined.

4. Add half of the herbs, then check the seasoning.

5. To serve, garnish with the remaining herbs, a drizzle of olive oil, and the Parmigiano-Reggiano cheese.

BAKED ZITI ☀ 🍁

PREP TIME: 20 MINUTES | COOK TIME: 35 MINUTES | READY IN: 55 MINUTES

Baked ziti is a simple and delicious pasta dish. With a terrific tomato sauce and lots of melted cheese and flavor, this was standard fare at my boyhood New Jersey home. This is Italian-American comfort food at its best.

MAKES 10 SERVINGS

½ pound whole wheat penne or ziti

5 cups Harvest Eating tomato sauce (page 282)

1½ cups whole-milk ricotta cheese

2 cups grated mozzarella cheese

¼ cup grated Parmesan cheese

1 tablespoon herbes de Provence (optional)

Kosher salt, to taste

Freshly ground black pepper, to taste

1. Cook the pasta according to package directions. Drain, run under cold water for a couple minutes, and set aside.

2. Preheat the oven to 350°F.

3. Combine the cooked pasta, 2 cups of the tomato sauce, and the ricotta cheese in a large bowl and mix well.

4. Place a layer of the pasta in a 2-quart casserole dish, add a layer of the tomato sauce, mozzarella cheese, Parmesan cheese, herbes de Provence, salt, and pepper.

5. Repeat the layers, ending with a topping of the mozzarella cheese.

6. Bake for 35 minutes or until bubbly and the cheese has melted and is starting to brown.

GRILLED VEGETABLES NAPOLEON ☀

PREP TIME: 10 MINUTES | COOK TIME: 20 MINUTES | READY IN: 30 MINUTES

This is a great way to use up abundant summertime vegetables. For this recipe I like to use bell peppers, zucchini, and eggplant that are abundant at summer farmer's markets and in my garden. It makes an elegant side dish, too.

MAKES 4 SERVINGS

2 whole bell peppers, sliced

1 red onion, sliced

1 zucchini, sliced

1 eggplant, sliced

1 summer squash, sliced

3 portobello mushrooms

¾ cup pure olive oil

Kosher salt, to taste

Freshly ground black pepper, to taste

2 tablespoons Harvest Eating House Seasoning (page 278)

½ (8-ounce) mozzarella cheese ball, sliced

1. Toss the peppers, onion, zucchini, eggplant, squash and mushrooms in a bowl with the olive oil, salt, pepper, and seasoning mix.

2. Grill the vegetables on the stovetop in a grill pan or on a gas or charcoal grill until nice grill marks appear. Preheat the oven to 350°F.

3. Layer the grilled vegetables with slices of cheese (in between every two vegetables) in a stack and secure with a toothpick. Place on a baking sheet in the oven and roast for 3 minutes.

BOWTIE PASTA WITH BUTTERNUT SQUASH ❦

PREP TIME: 10 MINUTES | COOK TIME: 20 MINUTES | READY IN: 30 MINUTES

This fall-inspired dish is a classic in Italian culture. The simplicity and lack of a red sauce bedazzles many Americans. The addition of the browned butter (beurre noisette) sage sauce is sinful and unique.

MAKES 6 SERVINGS

1 (16-ounce) box bowtie pasta

1 large butternut squash, peeled, seeded, and chopped

½ pound (2 sticks) unsalted butter

2 teaspoons lemon zest

1 tablespoon fresh sage leaves, chopped, ½ teaspoon reserved for garnish

¼ teaspoon kosher salt

¼ teaspoon freshly grated black pepper

3 tablespoons Parmigiano-Reggiano cheese, finely grated

1. Prepare the pasta according to the package directions.

2. Boil the butternut squash in about 4 cups water over high heat for about 5 minutes. Drain and cool under running water for a couple minutes.

3. Melt the butter in a skillet over medium-low heat. Cook the butter until it starts to brown and smells nutty and toasted.

4. Remove the butter from the heat and add the zest, sage, salt, and pepper.

5. Toss the cooked squash and pasta in the butter sauce.

6. Serve topped with the grated cheese and garnish with the reserved sage leaves.

HARVEST EATING LASAGNA ❦

PREP TIME: 40 MINUTES | COOK TIME: 45 MINUTES | READY IN: I HOUR 25 MINUTES

This fabulous twist on classic lasagna is perfect for cold weather months when hearty ingredients are bountiful. This recipe uses butternut squash, kale, leeks, sweet potatoes and a classic French mother sauce called béchamel. It's certainly a favorite recipe on HarvestEating.com.

MAKES 8 SERVINGS

2 pounds kale

1 pound leeks, sliced

2 garlic cloves, minced

2 tablespoons pure olive oil

Harvest Eating House Seasoning (page 278), to taste

1 (16-ounce) package lasagna

6 cups béchamel sauce (page 284)

2 whole sweet potatoes, thinly sliced

2 cups shredded Gruyère cheese

2 cups shredded fresh mozzarella

1. Preheat the oven to 350°F.

2. Thoroughly wash the kale and leeks with warm water in large bowl. Submerge the greens, gently moving them in the water. Pour out the water and repeat the process at least three times or until all the grit is removed. Drain in a colander.

3. Steam the kale for about 10 minutes until softened and reduced. It should be about 3 cups of cooked kale.

4. Trim the tops of the leeks. To cook the leeks, add the olive oil to a large sauté pan over medium-high heat. Cook the leeks along with the garlic for about 3 minutes and season with Harvest Eating House Seasoning; cook for an additional 2 minutes and set aside to cool.

5. Assemble the lasagna in layers in a 13 x 9-inch baking dish. Start with the lasagna and cover the bottom of the dish. Add some sauce and then layer as follows: kale, raw sweet potatoes, leeks, Gruyère, and mozzarella. Repeat the layers until the dish is about full, ending with cheese.

6. Bake until bubbly and starting to brown on top or until the sweet potatoes are tender when tested with a fork, 35 to 40 minutes.

PASTA WITH CAULIFLOWER AND KALE-ALMOND PESTO ✳

PREP TIME: 30 MINUTES | COOK TIME: 10 MINUTES | READY IN: 40 MINUTES

My unique Kale-Almond Pesto is used to make this wonderful wintertime pasta dish. Roasted cauliflower brings a nice texture and the orange zest cuts through to balance the flavors. This is a very interesting recipe.

MAKES 4 SERVINGS

5 tablespoons extra-virgin olive oil, divided

1 cup chopped roasted cauliflower

½ cup roasted shallots, peeled and whole

½ pound whole wheat penne pasta (cooked according to package instructions)

¼ cup kale pesto (page 240)

2 tablespoons minced fresh chives, divided

1 teaspoon chopped orange zest

1 tablespoon freshly squeezed orange juice

3 tablespoons grated Parmesan cheese

1 teaspoon kosher salt

½ teaspoon freshly ground black pepper

1. Heat 3 tablespoons of the olive oil in a large skillet over medium heat. Add the cauliflower and shallots. Sauté them for 2 minutes; then add the cooked pasta.

2. Add the kale pesto and sauté, stirring often to prevent sticking. Add 1 tablespoon of the chives and the orange zest and continue stirring.

3. Add the orange juice, Parmesan cheese, salt, and pepper.

4. Arrange the pasta on a serving dish and top with more cheese and chives and finish the dish with a drizzle of olive oil.

Chef's Note: To roast cauliflower and shallots, remove the cauliflower florets and place them in a roasting pan with the unpeeled shallots. Toss to coat with oil, season with salt and pepper, and roast in a 375-degree oven for 15 minutes.

8 | SAUCES, SPREADS, DRESSINGS, AND OILS

SUN-DRIED CHERRY VINAIGRETTE ✳

Cherries are in season in late spring throughout the upper Midwest and are not only delicious, but healthy too. This is my favorite vinaigrette recipe. The cherries are amazing when paired with blue cheese in any salad. Try to find cherries that are not dried using sulfites.

MAKES 8 SERVINGS
OR 2 CUPS

½ cup sun-dried cherries

¼ cup red wine vinegar

2 tablespoons Dijon mustard

Pinch of kosher salt

Pinch of freshly ground black
    pepper

¾ cup pure olive oil

1. Place the cherries in a bowl and cover with boiling water. Let stand for 10 minutes.

2. Drain off most of the water and place in a blender with the vinegar, mustard, salt, and pepper. Blend for 15 seconds.

3. Turn off the blender. Remove the safety cap and, with the blender running, slowly drizzle in the oil to complete the emulsion.

ARTICHOKE TAPENADE ✳

PREP TIME: 15 MINUTES | COOK TIME: 5 MINUTES | READY IN: 20 MINUTES

Tapenade is usually made with olives. This is a variation on the theme. This is delicious on a piece of grilled fish, such as trout or sea bass.

MAKES 1½ CUPS

6 to 8 fresh artichokes, steamed
   and hearts removed

1 garlic clove, minced

Zest of ½ lemon

Juice of ½ lemon

1 tablespoon extra-virgin olive oil

1 teaspoon white wine or
   champagne vinegar

¼ teaspoon kosher salt

¼ teaspoon freshly ground
   black pepper

1. Combine all the ingredients in a food processor. Pulse until the mixture is spreadable.

2. Add more freshly ground black pepper to taste.

3. Tapenade can be stored in refrigerator for three days.

SESAME-CHIVE VINAIGRETTE ✳

PREP TIME: 5 MINUTES | READY IN: 5 MINUTES

This vinaigrette has many uses; from salads to sauces to marinades. Try this simple recipe and it will become a favorite of yours too.

MAKES 4 SERVINGS

2 tablespoons chopped fresh chives

¼ cup chopped fresh cilantro

1 teaspoon chopped fresh peeled ginger

1 garlic clove, chopped

1 teaspoon fish sauce

1 tablespoon toasted sesame oil

½ cup pure olive oil

3 tablespoons seasoned rice wine vinegar

1 tablespoon low-sodium soy sauce

Pinch of kosher salt

10 twists (¼ teaspoon) freshly ground black pepper

1. Combine the chives, cilantro, ginger, garlic, fish sauce, sesame oil, olive oil, vinegar, and soy sauce in a blender or jar with a tight-fitting lid.

2. Shake the jar vigorously, until the vinaigrette is emulsified.

3. If the mixture is too thick, add more vinegar, 1 tablespoon at a time.

4. Season with salt and pepper. If storing, shake to re-blend before using.

Chef's Note: An immersion blender works well here, too.

223 ∾ SAUCES, SPREADS, DRESSINGS, AND OILS

LEMON-THYME VINAIGRETTE ✺

PREP TIME: 5 MINUTES | READY IN: 5 MINUTES

Here is another simple vinaigrette to bring amazing clean and pure flavor to many dishes or salads. I use fresh thyme from my kitchen garden in this recipe. It serves as a sauce for roasted cod, too.

MAKES I CUP

1 garlic clove, minced

1 tablespoon chopped fresh
    thyme leaves

Juice of 1 lemon juice

2 tablespoons champagne
    vinegar

1 tablespoon Dijon mustard

½ cup pure olive oil

2½ tablespoons extra-virgin
    olive oil

Kosher salt, to taste

Freshly ground black pepper,
    to taste

1. Combine the garlic, thyme, lemon juice, vinegar, mustard, and oils in a blender or jar with a tight-fitting lid.

2. Shake the jar vigorously, until the vinaigrette is emulsified.

3. If the mixture is too thick, add more vinegar, 1 table-spoon at a time.

4. Season with salt and pepper. If storing, shake to re-blend before using.

Chef's Note: Lemon-thyme vinaigrette is simple to make and can be adjusted with other herbs such as basil, tarragon or chives.

SESAME-GINGER VINAIGRETTE ✳

This is a simple and delicious Asian-inspired vinaigrette to use for salad greens, steamed vegetables, on top of grilled fish or chicken or mixed into cooked rice.

**MAKES 6 SERVINGS
(ABOUT 1½ CUPS)**

1 garlic clove

3 tablespoons seasoned rice
wine vinegar

2 tablespoons freshly squeezed
lime juice

2 tablespoons minced fresh
ginger

4 tablespoons chopped fresh
cilantro

3 tablespoons minced shallots

Zest of 1 lime

5 tablespoons sesame oil

¾ cup pure or light olive oil

Pinch of kosher salt

Pinch of freshly ground black
pepper

1. Combine the garlic, vinegar, lime juice, ginger, cilantro, shallots, lime zest, and oils in a blender or jar with a tight-fitting lid.

2. Process in the blender at high speed or shake the jar vigorously, until the vinaigrette is emulsified.

3. If the mixture is too thick, add more vinegar, 1 tablespoon at a time.

4. Season with salt and pepper. If storing, shake to re-blend before using.

BASIL VINAIGRETTE ☀

This is a delicious and refreshing summer vinaigrette. Use fresh basil for this, and I recommend you grow your own. It's easy and all that much better. Use this vinaigrette on salads, fresh tomatoes, chicken and other grilled items.

MAKES 6 SERVINGS

2 cups fresh basil

½ shallot, coarsely chopped

1 garlic clove, coarsely chopped

2 tablespoons Dijon mustard

3 tablespoons red wine vinegar

9 tablespoons pure olive oil

Pinch of kosher salt

Pinch of freshly ground black pepper

1. Combine the basil, shallot, garlic, mustard, vinegar, and oil in a blender or jar with a tight-fitting lid.

2. Process in the blender at high speed, or shake the jar vigorously, until the vinaigrette is emulsified.

3. If the mixture is too thick, add more vinegar, 1 tablespoon at a time.

4. Season with salt and pepper. If storing, shake to re-blend before using.

MANGO SALSA ☀

Mango salsa with fresh cilantro, shallots, chipotle peppers, and lime juice provides a fresh, tropical taste for your next Latin-inspired meal. It's perfect on grilled fish, such as Mahi Mahi, or for snacking with tortilla chips.

MAKES 2 SERVINGS

½ fresh mango, diced

3 tablespoons chopped fresh cilantro

Pinch of Harvest Eating House Seasoning (page 278)

½ chipotle pepper or other hot chile pepper, diced

Juice of 1 lime

½ cup diced organic tomato

½ small shallot, diced

1. Combine the mango, cilantro, Harvest Eating House Seasoning, pepper, lime juice, tomato, and shallot in a bowl. Mix well.

2. Serve with tortilla chips.

Chef's Note: Jalapeños work well too. Habaneros are extremely hot, so if you use them you might want to reduce the amount as desired.

SIMPLE SALSA FRESCA ☀

PREP TIME: 15 MINUTES | MARINATING TIME: 15 MINUTES | READY IN: 30 MINUTES

Classic tomato salsa fresca is a year-round favorite in Mexico. It's delicious, fresh, and easy to prepare. This often makes an appearance at summer cocktail parties and certainly Mexican night at our house.

MAKES 2 CUPS

3 vine ripe tomatoes, diced

1 jalapeño pepper, minced

1 large bunch fresh cilantro, chopped

Juice of 2 limes

1 small white onion, minced

1 teaspoon olive oil

Kosher salt, to taste

A few twists of freshly ground black pepper

1. Combine the tomatoes, jalapeño pepper, cilantro, lime juice, onion, olive oil, salt and pepper in a bowl; mix well.

2. Serve with organic blue tortilla chips.

Chef's Note: Only add the salt if you are serving the salsa right away. If not, add the salt 10 minutes before serving. For less spice, remove the seeds from the jalapeño pepper.

BASIL-WALNUT PESTO ☀

PREP TIME: 10 MINUTES | READY IN: 10 MINUTES

This is a delicious spin on the classic pesto in which the pine nuts are replaced by walnuts. Walnuts are high in healthy omega-3 oils, and have a fuller flavor.

MAKES 1½ CUPS

2 bunches fresh basil

½ cup fresh walnuts

1 garlic clove

4 tablespoons Parmigiano-Reggiano cheese

Pinch of kosher salt

Pinch of freshly ground black pepper

¾ cup extra-virgin olive oil

1. Combine the basil, walnuts, and garlic in a food processor. Process on low to start breaking down the basil leaves. While running on low, add the cheese, salt, and pepper.

2. Turn off the processor and scrape down the sides of the bowl before adding the oil; then turn the processor back on and slowly drizzle in the olive oil while the processor is running.

3. Reseason if needed with additional salt and pepper.

Chef's Note: Use this pesto on pasta, in soup, on crisp bread or on grilled fish or chicken. Buy good quality oil. Inexpensive supermarket olive oil will give terrible results. It's all about the oil.

HABANERO PEACH JAM ☀

This is a delicious and spicy concoction of peaches, cilantro, habanero pepper and citrus vinegar that makes a great topping for hearty grilled foods, such as pork tenderloin or grilled chicken.

MAKES 6 SERVINGS

3 yellow freestone peaches, peeled, pitted, and diced

¼ cup granulated sugar

2 tablespoons chopped fresh cilantro

¼ teaspoon minced habanero pepper

Pinch of kosher salt

5 twists of freshly ground black pepper

2 teaspoons citrus champagne vinegar

1. Combine the peaches, sugar, cilantro, habanero pepper, salt, black pepper, and vinegar in a saucepan and bring to simmer over medium-low heat.

2. Cover, reduce the heat to very low, and cook for 15 minutes. After 15 minutes, mash the mixture well with a potato masher.

3. Cool completely on a sheet pan or in a separate bowl. The sheet pan allows for quicker cooling.

4. Serve at room temperature.

Chef's Note: You can substitute apple cider vinegar for the champagne vinegar. Free-stone peaches are late season peaches and the pit is removeable.

ROSEMARY AND LEMON-INFUSED OIL ☀

PREP TIME: 5 MINUTES | COOK TIME: 30 SECONDS | READY IN: 6 MINUTES

The secret to making a great-tasting flavored oil is to not have the oil too hot or the herbs will be bitter. Infused oils are great to use in marinades, on pizzas, to cook eggs, and so much more.

MAKES 8 SERVINGS

½ cup pure olive oil

1 tablespoon chopped fresh rosemary (no stems)

1 garlic clove, sliced

Zest of 1 lemon

Pinch of gray sea salt

A few twists of black pepper

1. Warm the oil in a saucepan over medium-low heat.

2. Add the rosemary, garlic, lemon zest, salt, and pepper.

3. Sizzle for 30 seconds then pour into a glass bowl.

CRANBERRY-ORANGE COMPOTE 🍁

PREP TIME: 15 MINUTES | COOK TIME: 35 MINUTES | READY IN: 50 MINUTES

Make this delicious compote during your next holiday season. The simple flavors of orange and nutmeg are the perfect counterpart to the tartness of real cranberries. This is a great complement to the roasted turkey on your holiday plate. It can be made weeks ahead then frozen to make holiday meal preparations easier. Also, it makes a colorful ready-to-serve holiday gift.

MAKES 20 SERVINGS

1 pound whole cranberries

Juice and zest of 1 navel orange

¼ teaspoon freshly grated nutmeg (c'mon man, grate your own!)

1½ cups sugar

1. Combine the cranberries, orange juice and zest, nutmeg, and sugar in a heavy-bottomed pot over medium high.

2. After it comes to a boil turn the heat to low and cook for about 35 minutes until the berry skins burst and mixture reduces by about one-third.

3. Remove from the heat and allow to cool; it will thicken as it cools.

Chef's Note: To cool faster, place the pot in the sink then fill the sink with cold water about halfway up the sides of the pot (not in the pot) and stir occasionally.

CRANBERRY VINAIGRETTE 🍁

Cranberry vinaigrette is very easy to make and great on grilled chicken or garden fresh greens. I also use this recipe as a sauce for grilled pork tenderloin on fall and winter nights. The tartness of the cranberries cuts through the fat of grilled meats.

MAKES 8 SERVINGS

½ cup dried cranberries

2 tablespoons Dijon mustard

2 tablespoons minced shallots

¼ cup red wine vinegar

½ cup pure or light olive oil

¼ cup extra-virgin olive oil

½ teaspoon kosher salt

A few twists of freshly ground
   black pepper

1. Place the cranberries in a bowl and cover with boiling water; then cover with plastic wrap. Allow to re-hydrate for 20 minutes; then drain.

2. Combine the cranberries, mustard, shallots, vinegar, and oils in a blender or jar with a tight-fitting lid.

3. Process in the blender at high speed, or shake the jar vigorously, until the vinaigrette is emulsified.

4. If the mixture is too thick, add more vinegar, 1 tablespoon at a time.

5. Season with salt and pepper. If storing, shake to re-blend before using.

POMEGRANATE VINAIGRETTE ✸

PREP TIME: 3 MINUTES | COOK TIME: 5 MINUTES | READY IN: 8 MINUTES

Pomegranates are known for health benefits—they contain antioxidants that may fight cancer. This makes a great sauce as well; it can be used on grilled fish or chicken.

MAKES 10 SERVINGS

¾ cup pomegranate juice
  concentrate

1 tablespoon Dijon mustard

1 small shallot, minced

1 garlic clove, minced

1 tablespoon freshly squeezed
  lemon juice

2 tablespoons extra-virgin
  olive oil

¼ cup pure olive oil

Pinch of kosher salt

Freshly ground black pepper,
  to taste

1. Cook the pomegranate juice in a small saucepan over medium-high heat until it reduces to ¼ cup; allow to cool.

2. Combine the pomegranate juice, mustard, shallot, garlic and lemon juice, and oils in a blender or jar with a tight-fitting lid.

3. Process in the blender at high speed, or shake the jar vigorously, until the vinaigrette is emulsified.

4. Season with salt and pepper. If storing, shake to re-blend before using.

CRANBERRY SAUCE 🍁

PREP TIME: 10 MINUTES | COOK TIME: 45 MINUTES | READY IN: 55 MINUTES

Making cranberry sauce is a simple thing to do. The results, however, are wonderful on your palate. The tartness and background spice flavor is perfect against the turkey meat usually served alongside it.

MAKES 12 SERVINGS

2 (1-pound) bags fresh cranberries

1½ cups granulated sugar

¼ teaspoon ground nutmeg

¼ teaspoon ground cinnamon

¼ teaspoon ground cloves

Juice and zest of 2 medium oranges

1 teaspoon kosher salt

1. Place the cranberries in a heavy-bottomed cooking pot. Add the sugar, nutmeg, cinnamon and cloves to the cranberries.

2. Add the orange zest and their juice.

3. Add in the salt and stir.

4. Cook the mixture on the stove over low heat for 45 minutes.

5. Pour the mixture onto a sheet pan and refrigerate to cool. The cranberries will thicken into a jelly-like consistency.

ORANGE HERB VINAIGRETTE ✳

PREP TIME: 10 MINUTES | READY IN: 10 MINUTES

This vinaigrette is versatile because you can use whatever herbs you have on hand. The orange juice brings it all together and helps to make it refreshing.

**MAKES 4 SERVINGS
OR 1 CUP**

½ tablespoon chopped fresh chives

½ tablespoon chopped fresh oregano

½ tablespoon chopped fresh thyme

½ tablespoon chopped fresh basil

Juice from 1 orange

1 tablespoon Dijon mustard

2 tablespoons rice wine vinegar

¼ cup pure olive oil

2 tablespoons extra-virgin olive oil

½ teaspoon kosher salt

½ teaspoon freshly ground black pepper

1. Combine the chives, oregano, thyme, basil, orange juice, mustard, vinegar, and oils in a blender or jar with a tight-fitting lid.

2. Process in the blender at high speed, or shake the jar vigorously, until the vinaigrette is emulsified.

3. If the mixture is too thick, add more vinegar, 1 tablespoon at a time.

4. Season with salt and pepper. If storing, shake to re-blend before using.

KALE-ALMOND PESTO ✻

PREP TIME: 10 MINUTES | READY IN: 10 MINUTES

Did you think pesto was just basil and pine nuts? Learn how to create a unique wintertime pesto from kale and almonds. This an awesome recipe worth trying for sure.

MAKES 6 SERVINGS OR 3 CUPS

1½ pounds kale (about 2 cups cooked)

½ cup almonds, toasted

2 tablespoons chopped shallots

1 garlic clove, chopped

4 tablespoons grated Parmigiano-Reggiano cheese

Kosher salt, to taste

Freshly ground black pepper, to taste

½ cup extra-virgin olive oil

1. In a stove top steamer with a couple cups of water in the bottom bring to a boil. Place the kale in the steamer, cover, and steam for about 10 minutes. Then, run the kale under cold water to stop the cooking process. Let it drain and set aside

2. Place the kale, almonds, shallots, garlic, cheese, salt and pepper in the bowl of a food processor.

3. Pulse several times to combine then drizzle in the olive oil.

4. Adjust seasoning to taste.

Chef's Note: Use this pesto on pasta, grilled meat or even pizza.

9 | DESSERTS AND DRINKS

FLOURLESS CHOCOLATE CAKE ❋❋❋❋

PREP TIME: 20 MINUTES | COOK TIME: 15 MINUTES
ASSEMBLY TIME: 10 MINUTES | READY IN: 45 MINUTES

This is the one recipe that speaks to my childhood like no other. My mother's flourless chocolate cake was served on every birthday, Thanksgiving, and Christmas during my childhood.

MAKES 8 SERVINGS

6 free-range eggs, separated

¾ cup granulated sugar

6 ounces 70% cacao chocolate

½ cup confectioners' sugar

¼ cup brewed espresso (or dark coffee)

1 pint heavy cream

1 teaspoon vanilla extract

1. Preheat the oven to 350°F. Coat a baking sheet with at least ½-inch sides with cooking spray, waxed paper, and then more cooking spray.

2. Beat the egg yolks with the granulated sugar in a medium bowl until fluffy and pale in color, about 5 minutes.

3. Beat the egg whites in a separate bowl until stiff peaks form.

4. Melt the chocolate in the top pan of a double boiler over hot water. Add the espresso or coffee. Remove from heat.

5. Slowly add a little of the chocolate mixture to the egg yolk mixture and mix well using a rubber spatula. Add the rest of chocolate mixture and mix well.

6. Add the egg whites in three additions being careful to fold them in to keep the batter light and airy.

7. Carefully pour the batter onto the prepared baking sheet and make sure it's as level as possible by tapping the sides and spreading with a spatula.

8. Place the baking sheet in the oven and cook for 10 minutes. Do not overcook. Remove from the oven and place a damp kitchen towel over the cooked cake and allow it to cool.

9. Using a chilled bowl and whisk, beat the heavy cream and vanilla extract, whipping the cream until it is thick.

10. Cut sheet cake in half, spread whipped cream between the layers; then chill in the refrigerator for 1½ hours. Add powdered sugar and strawberries before serving.

TIRAMISU ✺ ❋ ❋ ❀

Tiramisu is an Italian classic dessert. This dinner party favorite is surprisingly easy to make. The mascarpone cheese has a very unique flavor and texture and makes this dessert unforgettable.

MAKES 15 SERVINGS

4 free-range eggs, separated

½ cup granulated sugar

½ pint organic heavy cream

16 ounces mascarpone cheese, at room temperature

2 tablespoons Marsala wine

2 cups strong espresso coffee

1 package ladyfingers, crunchy style

Shaved chocolate, for garnish

1. Combine the egg yolks and the sugar in a bowl and whisk over a pot of simmering water (creating the effect of a double boiler). Whisk until the mixture reaches the ribbon stage *without* making scrambled eggs.

2. Whisk or beat the egg whites in a separate bowl until you have semi-stiff peaks. Set aside.

3. Whisk or beat the heavy cream in a separate bowl until it is very thick and stiff. Set aside.

4. Whisk the mascarpone cheese and heavy cream into the egg yolk and sugar mixture until it is well combined. Slowly fold in the egg whites to create an airy mixture. Set aside.

5. Add the Marsala wine to the strong coffee and then carefully and quickly soak each lady finger in the Marsala coffee mixture. Arrange one layer of ladyfingers in your serving dish.

6. Top with some of the cream mixture. Add a second layer of ladyfingers, top them with more cream mixture.

7. Finish with shaved chocolate. Using a vegetable peeler, peel a block of chocolate to make small curls. Put the curls on top of the tiramisu. Refrigerate for at least 4 hours before serving.

Chef's Note: Tiramisu contains partially cooked egg yolks and raw egg whites. It is not recommended for immune-compromised individuals, very young children or pregnant moms. If you can source eggs from pastured hens you'll have a MUCH better dessert as eggs are the main event here.

TIA MARIA'S PEANUT BUTTER BALLS ✸✳❄❈

PREP TIME: 10 MINUTES | COOK & CHILL TIME: 25 MINUTES | READY IN: 35 MINUTES

These peanut butter balls were created by my dear friend Tia who was with me when I began HarvestEating.com. They are easy to make and are a sure hit with kids. Healthy ingredients abound: dried fruit, flax seeds, coconut, oats, and peanut butter. Give them a try!

MAKES 12 SERVINGS

2 cups whole rolled oats

½ cup ground rolled oats

3 tablespoons ground organic golden flax seeds

1 cup dried fruit, such as raisins, cranberries, cherries or apricots

¼ cup organic coconut flakes

1 teaspoon vanilla extract

½ cup sunflower seeds

½ cup ground almonds

¼ cup pure olive oil

1 cup organic peanut butter

¼ cup honey

1. Place the first nine ingredients in a large work bowl (everything except peanut butter and honey).

2. In a small saucepan, heat the peanut butter and honey over medium-low heat until they become very viscous, about 5 minutes.

3. Add the warm peanut butter and honey mixture to the dry ingredients and mix well.

4. Mold the peanut butter mixture into balls the size of golf balls. For best results, refrigerate for 20 minutes before serving. Store them in an air-tight container in the refrigerator.

Chef's Note: Be sure to use organic peanut butter or Valencia peanut butter, which is low in pesticide residue. Also, be sure the nuts and dried fruit are fresh. These peanut butter balls are great for hiking or a natural snack for kids.

FIG CLAFOUTI ✺ ✺

PREP TIME: 20 MINUTES | COOK TIME: 20 MINUTES | READY IN: 40 MINUTES

This is a simple and delicious French-inspired dessert that classically is made with cherries that are very plentiful in central France. A simple batter is all that's needed to perfect this dish. It goes well with a sweet white wine from the Alsace region of France.

MAKES 6 SERVINGS

1 tablespoon cold organic
   unsalted butter

4 cups fresh figs, halved

½ cup sugar

4 medium free-range eggs

½ cup organic whole milk

3 tablespoons organic unsalted
   butter, melted

1 cup all-purpose flour

Pinch of kosher salt

1. Preheat the oven to 325°F.

2. Grease a round shallow pie plate with the cold butter.

3. Arrange the figs in the pie plate, some cut side up, some cut side down. The plate should be crowded with figs.

4. Combine the sugar, eggs, milk, and melted butter in a large bowl or food processor. Process until the ingredients are well mixed. Then add the flour and salt. Your batter should be thick but pourable.

5. Pour the batter over the figs and bake until the batter is set and slightly golden brown. Serve at room temperature.

RICE PUDDING WITH DRIED CHERRIES *

This rustic rice pudding with delicate dried cherries and a touch of maple syrup is a cold weather favorite at the Snow household. Aside from the syrup there is no sugar added. This dish makes me very happy!

MAKES 8 SERVINGS

2 cups uncooked rice
(short grain)

3 cups organic whole milk

1 whole vanilla bean, split

1 cup dried cherries

2 teaspoons real maple syrup

1. Cook the rice according to package directions. Add the milk, vanilla bean, and cherries.

2. Cover and cook over low heat, stirring occasionally, until the milk is absorbed and the rice is creamy.

3. Serve with a splash of syrup or a dollop of Greek-style yogurt.

BANANAS WITH
ROASTED HAZELNUTS AND GANACHE ✳

PREP TIME: 5 MINUTES | READY IN: 5 MINUTES

Ganache is the star of this show, dressing this interesting, yet simple dessert. Be sure the hazelnuts are fresh and the bananas are not overripe.

MAKES 2 SERVINGS

2 whole organic bananas

¼ cup toasted hazelnuts

1 tablespoon caramel sauce (page 287)

2 tablespoons organic heavy cream

2 tablespoons chocolate ganache (page 288)

1. Slice the bananas in half and place on serving plates.

2. Toss a few hazelnuts onto each plate.

3. Top with the caramel sauce, cream, and ganache

SWEET POTATO CHEESECAKE ❧

PREP TIME: 30 MINUTES | COOK & CHILL TIME: 2½ HOURS | READY IN: 3 HOURS

This delicious and classic cheesecake has a Southern twist with the addition of roasted sweet potatoes. This is a very interesting dessert. The state of North Carolina is the leading producer of healthy sweet potatoes.

MAKES 12 SERVINGS

4 sweet potatoes, about
   1 pound total, peeled and
   quartered

2 cups graham cracker crumbs

8 tablespoons butter, melted

2 pounds (32 ounces) cream
   cheese, softened

1 cup sugar

Pinch of salt

5 large free-range eggs

2 egg yolks (from free-range
   eggs)

½ cup sour cream

3 tablespoons all-purpose flour

1 teaspoon vanilla extract

¼ teaspoon ground ginger

¼ teaspoon ground cinnamon

⅛ teaspoon grated fresh nutmeg

1. Preheat the oven to 450°F.

2. Place the sweet potatoes in a covered ovenproof baking dish and put in the oven. Roast the sweet potatoes for 15 to 20 minutes, or until fork-tender. Purée the roasted sweet potatoes in a blender or food processor.

3. To make the crust: Combine the graham cracker crumbs and melted butter in a bowl and mix well. Using a tablespoon, press this mixture into a 10-inch springform pan and chill for 30 minutes.

4. Put the cream cheese into the bowl of an electric mixer. Using the paddle attachment, beat until smooth. With the mixer running on medium speed, add the sugar and salt. Add the eggs and yolks one at a time, then add the sour cream, flour, vanilla, ginger, cinnamon, and nutmeg. Lower the mixer speed and add the sweet potato purée.

5. Pour the batter over the crust in the springform pan. Place the springform pan on the upper rack in the middle of the oven and an ovenproof dish of hot water on the lower rack under the cheesecake.

6. Bake at 450°F for 15 minutes; then reduce the oven temperature to 250°F and bake an additional 1½ hours, or until the center of the cheesecake is firm.

7. Cool the cheesecake on a rack for 30 minutes, then refrigerate until completely chilled.

PANETTONE BREAD PUDDING ❄

PREP TIME: 15 MINUTES | COOK TIME: 35 MINUTES | READY IN: 50 MINUTES

This bread pudding is awesome. The panettone really makes this a special dessert. Panettone is a classic, Christmastime fruit-stuffed bread that is very popular in Italy. This is not your bricklike fruitcake. This dense, eggy bread is loaded with candied citrus and other fruits. It rocks when made into bread pudding!

MAKES 8 SERVINGS

4 large fresh free-range eggs

½ cup granulated sugar

2 tablespoons real maple syrup

3 cups organic whole milk

1 package panettone bread

1. Preheat the oven to 325°F.

2. Whisk the eggs and sugar together until pale yellow and well combined. Whisk in the maple syrup.

3. Add the milk and continue whisking until combined. Set aside.

4. Cut the bread into large cubes. Add the bread cubes to the milk mixture and mix well to make sure the bread is very wet.

5. Place the soaked bread cubes in a buttered, 2-quart casserole dish and bake in the oven until lightly browned on top, 35 to 45 minutes.

Chef's Note: Serve with ice cream.

CHOCOLATE ESPRESSO POTS DU CRÈME ✳

PREP TIME: 15 MINUTES | COOK & CHILL TIME: 3¾ HOURS | READY IN: 4 HOURS

Chocolate espresso pots du crème are intensely flavored and rich with the flavor of high quality chocolate and a hint of espresso. Simple to make, these desserts are a show-stopper. I like desserts like this because the sugar used is minimal, allowing the flavors of chocolate to come through.

MAKES 8 SERVINGS

8 ounces bittersweet chocolate

1 cup organic heavy cream

⅓ cup organic milk

¾ cup espresso powder

Pinch of kosher salt

6 free-range egg yolks

2 tablespoons granulated sugar

1. Put the oven rack in middle position and preheat the oven to 300°F.

2. Place the chocolate in a heat-proof bowl.

3. In a small heavy saucepan, bring the cream, milk, espresso powder, and salt just to a boil, stirring until the espresso powder is dissolved. Pour the mixture over the chocolate, whisking until the chocolate is melted and mixture is smooth.

4. In another bowl, whisk together the egg yolks, sugar, and salt. Add warm chocolate mixture to this in a slow stream, whisking constantly. Pour the combined custard through a fine-mesh sieve into a 1-quart bowl with a pour spout.

5. Line the bottom of a baking pan (large enough to hold 8 ramekins) with a folded kitchen towel and arrange the ramekins on the towel. Divide the chocolate mixture among the ramekins. Poke several holes in a large sheet of foil with a skewer and cover the ramekins tightly with foil. Add water to the baking pan to make a hot water bath or bain marie. Bake until the pots du crème are set around edges but still slightly wobbly in their centers, 30 to 35 minutes.

6. Transfer the ramekins to a rack to cool completely, uncovered, about 1 hour. (Custards will set as they cool.) Then chill, covered, until cold, at least 3 hours.

Chef's Note: Can be made up to three days ahead.

MANGO CRÈME BRÛLÉE ✳

PREP TIME: 15 MINUTES | COOK & CHILL TIME: 3 HOURS | READY IN: 3¼ HOURS

Crème brûlée is a famous little French dessert that all too often has too much sugar. I prefer using less so I can taste the velvet mouth feel and scent of vanilla without the sugar bomb. It's a perfect dessert for a special evening. Can be made ahead place in the dish then cooked to order.

MAKES 6 SERVINGS

2 cups organic heavy cream

1 whole vanilla bean, pods split

1 whole organic mango, peeled, seeded, and diced

6 organic or farm fresh egg yolks

½ cup granulated sugar, plus 2 tablespoons for dusting

1. Preheat the oven to 325°F.

2. Combine the cream and vanilla beans with split pods in a saucepot.

3. Heat the mixture over medium heat until it scalds, just under the boiling point. Watch so it does not boil over!

4. Place a few pieces of the diced mango into each custard cup or ramekin.

5. Combine the egg yolks and the ½ cup sugar in a bowl. Beat until smooth and pale yellow, about 5 minutes.

6. Temper the egg yolks by whisking in a small amount of the hot cream mixture. Repeat that process twice, then add all of the remaining cream to the egg mixture.

7. Fill the custard cups three-quarters full with the mixture. Place the filled cups in a large rimmed pan. Add hot water to the pan reaching halfway up the sides of the custard cups.

8. Bake for 35 minutes or until the custard is just set but still giggling slightly. Cool for 25 minutes, then refrigerate until well chilled, about 2 hours.

9. Dust the surface of each custard cup with 1 teaspoon sugar. Place under a hot broiler or use a blow torch to brûlée the tops which means to slightly burn the sugar so it gets brown.

STRAWBERRY-BANANA SHAKE ✲

PREP TIME: 3 MINUTES | READY IN: 3 MINUTES

This simple and nutritious milkshake with banana and ripe strawberries contains plain yogurt and flaxseed to enhance the nutritional punch. This is a staple morning breakfast for me when local strawberries are in season. Substitute any local berry in this recipe.

MAKES 2 SERVINGS

1 medium banana

½ cup fresh ripe strawberries

2 cups organic whole milk

½ cup organic plain yogurt

2 tablespoons ground organic golden flaxseed

1. Put the banana, strawberries, milk, yogurt, and flaxseed into the blender.

2. Purée until well mixed.

3. Pour into a glass and enjoy.

Chef's Note: It's easy to double, triple, or quadruple this recipe when serving your friends.

CHERRY VANILLA MILKSHAKE ☀

PREP TIME: 5 MINUTES | READY IN: 5 MINUTES

This is a quick-and-easy, low-carb breakfast milkshake with protein powder, cherries, and banana. I make this in late spring with fresh tart cherries.

MAKES 2 SERVINGS

¾ cup fresh tart cherries

2 cups organic whole milk

2 scoops natural vanilla whey protein powder

½ small organic banana

1. Combine the frozen cherries, milk, protein power, and banana in a blender.

2. Blend at high speed for 1 minute.

3. Pour into a glass and enjoy.

Chef's Note: Flax seed is a nice, healthy addition.

BLUEBERRY COCONUT SMOOTHIE ☀

PREP TIME: 5 MINUTES | READY IN: 5 MINUTES

A healthy blueberry coconut smoothie with almonds and Jersey cow's milk is a perfect summertime treat. I serve this smoothie quite often during blueberry season, which is late spring/early summer in western North Carolina.

MAKES 2 SERVINGS

½ cup blueberries

¼ cup organic coconut flakes, unsweetened

1 tablespoon sliced almonds

2 cups organic whole or soy milk

Ice cubes (optional)

1. Combine blueberries, coconut flakes, almonds, milk, and ice cubes, if using, in a blender.

2. Purée until smooth.

3. Pour into a glass and enjoy.

LEMONADE ☀

PREP TIME: 2 MINUTES | COOK TIME: 5 MINUTES | READY IN: 7 MINUTES

Forget the powdered stuff. Learn how to make delicious fresh-squeezed lemonade using this easy method. There is no better drink on a hot summer day than this.

MAKES 8 SERVINGS

¼ cup granulated sugar

¼ cup hot water

Juice of 4 large organic lemons

½ gallon cold water

1. Create a simple syrup by dissolving the sugar in the hot water.

2. Strain the lemon juice and add to the simple syrup. Add the cold water; mix well.

3. Pour over ice and enjoy!

Chef's Note: This recipe yields about a half-gallon of lemonade. A large Mason jar with a lid works well to mix the ingredients.

SWEET TEA ☀

PREP TIME: 5 MINUTES | STEEPING TIME: 5 MINUTES | READY IN: 10 MINUTES

Too many people drink junk sugar chemical tea. It's so easy to make good tea at home. This one adds the interesting flavor and nutritional punch Rooibos tea provides. This is always in our refrigerator in warm months.

MAKES 8 CUPS

½ gallon cold water, divided

¼ cup Rooibos tea leaves

2 large black tea bags (each bag should make 32 ounces of tea)

2 tablespoons granulated sugar

1. Bring 2 cups of the water to boil over high heat. Pour the boiling water into a large pot over the Rooibos tea leaves, the tea bags and the sugar.

2. Stir and let steep for 10 minutes.

3. Remove the tea bags and then the strain the concentrated mixture into a pitcher containing the rest of the cold water.

Chef's Note: This method of brewing ice tea is more efficient than bringing the entire ½ gallon of the water to a boil. When you do that, you have to wait until it cools or add ice, which dilutes the tea.

MANGO LASSI ☀

In the country of India, this is very popular as a smoothie-type beverage with a special use—cooling the palette after a spicy meal. I like to use very ripe mangos and unsweetened coconut cream. You can find coconut cream concentrate in either the ethnic food or Asian aisle of your organic grocery store.

MAKES 2 (8-OUNCE)
SERVINGS

2 cups organic coconut milk

1 ripe mango, cut into large chunks

2 tablespoons coconut cream concentrate (optional)

½ cup plain yogurt

1. Combine the coconut milk, mango, coconut cream concentrate, if using, and yogurt in a blender.

2. Process until smooth.

3. Pour into a glass and enjoy. This is best enjoyed cold.

PART III | COOKONOMICS

10. BE INSPIRED

WHAT IS COOKONOMICS?

A TERM COINED BY MY COOKBOOK editor, but claimed by me, *cookonomics* simply means using the principles of home economics to make healthy, cost-effective replacements for store-bought pantry items and goods. Cookonomics is a practice that is at the very core of Harvest Eating. Like I mentioned earlier in the book, in years gone by people used principles of preservation and kitchen ingenuity to make many of the items most of us buy from stores today.

It is my desire that everyone reading this book would try to make some of these staple recipes at home to break the cycle of relying on so many premade, store-bought items. This is especially important given the amount of fillers, preservatives, and questionable ingredients that are pervasive in many popular packaged foods. I am quite confident that you will improve your overall health by taking matters into your own hands whenever possible. It's time we take back the responsibility of feeding ourselves and feeding our families.

∾ HOW IS IT DONE? ∾

T HERE ARE MANY GREAT EXAMPLES of cookonomics, but let's start by using this simple illustration: sour cream. It was only at the beginning of the last century that premade goods became available and only in the cities. Before then people had to make their own sour cream. A bacteria was mixed with fresh cream and the development of lactic acid produced a tangy flavor and thick texture. In France, and many other cultures, thickened sour creams are quite popular, and lucky for us, can be easily made at home by combining heavy cream with a little cultured buttermilk or yogurt. It takes only twenty-four hours at roughly seventy degrees to produce something with far more flavor than store-bought sour cream, and it costs much less too. I will never forget my first trip to a Mexican market in Puerto Vallarta where they had big vats of thickened cream sitting in the open air ready to be ladled out and taken home. It was quite a sight to behold.

You can save money, have fun, and produce healthier and better tasting foods at home with your own carefully selected ingredients and know-how. If you dine at my house, you will most likely *not* see a bottle of commercial salad dressing, store-bought pickles, branded crème fraîche, boxed pancake mix, or de-hydrated potato flakes. These are all items that are easily made at home that you and your family can regularly enjoy.

One of the keys to successful cookonomics is being properly prepared before you start. It makes no sense to make a quarter cup of vinaigrette for example, when making five cups takes no more effort or time. Also, I would never cook a quarter pound of pasta. Instead, I cook the entire pound and store any leftovers for later use. So before you start, plan ahead. Be ready to store your staples. For example, when making a vinaigrette, make enough to fill a large squirt bottle or dressing jar. Vinaigrettes keep well due to their high acid content, so they will be happy in the refrigerator until you finish them. When making pancake mix, make enough to freeze in batches. I make about three pounds at a time and store it in several freezer bags for later use. We usually get six month's of use out of one batch, and the last bag tastes as good as the first. To be successful you must make the best use of your time, which means making a few pounds at a time. It's worth all the effort, though. Our homemade pancake mix is much healthier than store-bought, and is much cheaper when compared to the boxed stuff. In exchange for a little labor, you are bolstering your health, your taste, and your budget. This is why I am so passionate about the cookonomics principles. After you try a few recipes on your own, you will be too. I regularly post new how-to videos and recipes to the Cookonomics section of www.harvesteating.com so you can easily reference them.

11. DO IT YOURSELF

WHY SHOULD YOU GRIND YOUR own meat and make your own yogurt?

Ask yourself these questions: Do you know exactly what's in there? Do you know the integrity of the people who produced the product? Is the plant clean? Are the products *still* made the same way as when you first tried them? Or has the company cut back and starting using inferior ingredients to squeeze every cent of profit out? These are all good questions and ones that may be impossible, or at lest very hard, to find the answers to when talking about yogurt or ground beef. If you are fortunate enough to have a local butcher you can trust, then go ahead and buy the ground meat. For the other 99 percent of the country, read on.

Federal regulations are a bit ambiguous at times when it comes to food. Meat manufacturers and dairies are allowed to have a certain percentage of "foreign materials" in the products they make. That is enough for me to do cookonomics. The benefits of making your own staples is that you can save money and have control over the freshness and quality of what you are making. There are also flavor benefits. Add some homegrown berries to your yogurt or different cuts of beef to help flavor your burger. Mix up some spices and ground pork and you've made your own sausage. The possibilities are infinite.

Jumping into cookonmoics takes some preparation because you'll need certain supplies and equipment, nothing fancy or expensive, though. If you want to make your own salad dressing, it will be helpful to have a blender or immersion blender, and you'll need proper storing containers (a jar with a tight-fitting lid like a mason jar) and a serving device (such as a cruet). When making yogurt, however, you'll need storage jars and a thermometer.

I suggest picking a few things to try first: yogurt, salad dressing, and pancake mixes. Get your kids involved; they will have a blast helping, and surely they will be more eager to eat what they had a hand in making. Some of my favorite cookonomics items are: sauerkraut, crème frâiche, sausage, ricotta cheese, jams and jellies, demi glace, and hand-ground flours, such as whole wheat.

HOMEMADE YOGURT

PREP TIME: 10 MINUTES | COOKING TIME: 60 MINUTES | TOTAL TIME: 70 MINUTES

MAKES ABOUT 4 QUARTS

1 gallon whole milk
(preferably raw)

8 ounces plain yogurt
(check the date for freshness)

1. Start by sterilizing everything you will need: a heavy-bottomed pot, thermometer, a small bowl, measuring cups, 16 8-ounce jars for storage, whisks and spoons, lids, thermometer, and an insulated cooler.

2. Prepare your insulated cooler (if you do not have a yogurt maker) by adding a gallon of 105-degree water and closing the lid.

3. In a heavy-bottom pot bring the milk to 190 degrees over medium heat. Turn off the heat and let the milk cool to 105 degrees.

4. In a small bowl mix together the yogurt and 8 ounces of the 105-degree milk (to temper the yogurt).

5. Return the milk-yogurt mixture to the remaining milk. Stir to incorporate.

6. Fill sixteen sterilized 8-ounce mason jars with the warm cultured milk. Place lids on the jars, and place the jars in the preheated cooler.

7. Close the lid and set in a warm area for 4 to 6 hours.

8. Remove the jars from the water and refrigerate the yogurt. It will keep in the refrigerator for up to three weeks.

Chef's Note: To add fruit to your yogurt, cook one pound chopped fresh fruit and a tablespoon of sugar in a saucepan over low heat until reduced by about half. Let it cool. Pour about a quarter cup of fruit into each jar before pouring the hot milk on top.

HEALTHY PANCAKE MIX

PREP TIME: 2 MINUTES | READY IN: 2 MINUTES

Learn how to make your own homemade (and very healthy) pancake mix. We keep this mix on hand all year long and pair it with fresh fruit in the summer or frozen fruit throughout the year for a great Sunday morning breakfast treat. Try to find flour that is as fresh as possible. Some health food stores carry stone-ground flour, which is oftentimes organic and delicious. You don't want flour that has been sitting around. To really give yourself a treat, try buying from Anson Mills (www.ansonmills.com). Tell Glenn Roberts I sent you.

MAKES 12 SERVINGS

1 cup whole wheat flour

1 cup unbleached all-purpose flour

1 cup rye flour

1 cup corn meal

2 tablespoons granulated sugar

2 teaspoons baking powder

1 teaspoon kosher salt

1. Combine the flours, corn meal, sugar, baking powder, and salt in a large, sealable plastic freezer bag.

2. Store the mix in the freezer until ready to use.

Chef's Note: For 3 to 4 servings, combine 1 cup of the pancake mix with 1½ cups milk and 1 egg. Pour the batter on a hot griddle and cook on each side until golden brown.

CAESAR DRESSING

PREP TIME: 5 MINUTES | READY IN: 5 MINUTES

Learn how to make a simple and delicious homemade Caesar salad dressing. Most store-bought salad dressings are a joke. They're loaded with preservatives, cheap oil, and lots of salt. I always make dressings and vinaigrettes at home and hope you will too. It's one of the basic tenets of Harvest Eating.

MAKES 8 SERVINGS

2 tablespoons minced shallots

3 tablespoons grated Parmesan cheese

2 garlic cloves

2 tablespoons mayonnaise

2 teaspoons Dijon mustard

1 teaspoon Worcestershire sauce

1 teaspoon dried oregano

1 teaspoon fish sauce

2 tablespoons red wine vinegar

¾ cup pure olive oil

Kosher salt, to taste

Freshly ground black pepper, to taste

1. Combine the shallots, cheese, garlic, mayonnaise, mustard, Worcestershire sauce, oregano, fish sauce and vinegar in a blender or food processor.

2. With the blender running, slowly add the oil and continue processing until emulsified.

3. Season with salt and pepper.

Chef's Note: Caesar salad dressing is also a delicious marinade for meats, chicken, or even firm-fleshed fish. I use fish sauce instead of anchovies for a better flavor.

BALSAMIC REDUCTION

PREP TIME: 1 MINUTE | COOK TIME: 25 MINUTES | READY IN: 26 MINUTES

Reduced balsamic vinegar is a syrupy concoction that makes a great garnish and adds rich flavor. Use it on grilled fruit, pasta, grilled meats, and much more. It is especially good drizzled over a chunk of good-quality Parmigiano-Reggiano cheese and strawberries.

MAKES 4 SERVINGS

¾ cups good-quality aged
    balsamic vinegar

1. Place the balsamic vinegar in shallow saucepan and bring to a simmer over medium-low heat. When simmering, reduce the heat to low and let the vinegar cook and reduce by two-thirds, about 25 minutes. Remove from the pot and cool to room temperature.

2. After the syrup has cooled it can be used in many ways. I love it on salads and grilled chicken, and with my Harvest Eating Lasagna (page 217). Store in the refrigerator.

TARRAGON RED WINE VINEGAR

PREP TIME: 5 MINUTES | READY IN: 5 MINUTES

MAKES 4 CUPS

4 cups red wine vinegar

1 bunch fresh tarragon sprigs

3 whole cloves

5 peppercorns

2 allspice berries

1. Combine the vinegar, tarragon, cloves, peppercorns, and allspice in a large nonreactive pot. Bring to a boil over high heat.

2. Reduce the heat to medium low and simmer for about 10 minutes.

3. Let the vinegar cool completely and place in a jar with a tight-fitting lid.

Chef's Note: Add 2 to 3 drops of bleach to about 3 cups of water. Wash the herbs in the bleach solution for a few seconds, and then rinse well in fresh water. This helps to kill any microbes that may be lurking in the fresh tarragon. Use this technique for other herbs used in flavored oil.

FRENCH VINAIGRETTE

PREP TIME: 3 MINUTES | READY IN: 3 MINUTES

MAKES 1 CUP

2 tablespoons minced shallots

2 tablespoons Dijon mustard

¼ cup red wine vinegar

½ cup light or pure olive oil

¼ extra-virgin olive oil

½ teaspoon kosher salt

½ teaspoon fresh black pepper

1. Combine the shallots, mustard, vinegar, and oils in a blender or jar with a tight-fitting lid.

2. Process the blender at high speed, or shake the jar vigorously, until the vinaigrette is emulsified.

3. If the mixture is too thick, add more vinegar, 1 tablespoon at a time.

4. Season with salt and pepper. If storing, shake to re-blend before using.

SEASONAL BERRY VINAIGRETTE

PREP TIME: 15 MINUTES | READY IN: 15 MINUTES

MAKES 8 SERVINGS

1 cup fresh berries, rinsed (remove any stems)

1 heaping tablespoon Dijon mustard

2 tablespoons fresh minced shallots

6 tablespoons red wine vinegar

1 cup pure or light olive oil

Pinch of kosher salt

1 cup (about 15 twists) of freshly ground black pepper

1. Combine the berries, mustard, shallots, vinegar, and oil in a blender or jar with a tight-fitting lid.

2. Process in the blender at high speed, or shake the jar vigorously, until the vinaigrette is emulsified.

3. If the mixture is too thick, add more vinegar 1 tablespoon at a time.

4. Season with salt and pepper. If storing, shake to re-blend before using.

Chef's Note: You could substitute sunflower or safflower oil for the olive oil if you'd like.

BREAKFAST SAUSAGE

Breakfast sausage patties are easy to make and much better when done yourself. Learn how to make your own in less than ten minutes.

MAKES 10 SERVINGS

1 pound naturally-raised dark turkey meat, ground

1 pound naturally-raised pork, ground

2 tablespoons ground sage

1 teaspoon cayenne pepper (optional)

1 tablespoon Italian seasoning

1 tablespoon kosher salt

1 teaspoon freshly ground black pepper

1. Mix the turkey, pork, sage, cayenne pepper, Italian seasoning, salt, and black pepper together in bowl. Form the mixture into thin 2-ounce patties (about 2 inches in diameter).

2. Cook the patties on a skillet or griddle over medium heat until well caramelized and fully cooked—an internal temperature of 170°F.

Chef's Note: These can be made ahead and frozen. Buy the ingredients in bulk, and make a bunch to have on hand when you need them. This way you won't be forced to buy factory-farmed pork sausage.

FRESH PASTA

PREP TIME: 20 MINUTES | COOK TIME: 5 MINUTES | READY IN: 25 MINUTES

Unleash your inner Italian Grandma! Learn how to make fresh pasta from scratch. Find out why it tastes so much better fresh than boxed.

MAKES 4 SERVINGS

1¾ cups all-purpose flour

¼ cup whole wheat flour

4 eggs

2 tablespoons extra-virgin olive oil

1 tablespoon kosher salt

1. Combine the flours, eggs, olive oil, and salt in a large bowl. Mix well until a dough forms.

2. Turn out the dough onto a work surface.

3. Continue to knead in additional flour until the dough is no longer sticky, and is smooth.

4. Allow the dough to rest in the refrigerator for 30 minutes before cutting or shaping.

Chef's Note: Try to not overwork dough or it will become tough. You do not need to buy a pasta maker. Some stand mixers have pasta making attachments. Otherwise cutting the pasta with a knife, or, perhaps, with small cookie cutters will work just fine.

HOMEMADE PIZZA

PREP TIME: 90 MINUTES | COOK TIME: ABOUT 8 MINUTES | READY IN: 98 MINUTES

Making pizza is very easy with a few essential techniques, some good ingredients, and imagination. Pizza dough can easily be made in bulk and frozen. Good tomato sauce for a pizza is critical.

MAKES 2 (10-INCH) PIZZAS

PIZZA SAUCE

½ cup extra-virgin olive oil

5 garlic cloves, minced

1 small shallot, minced

1 (28-ounce) can organic plum tomatoes, undrained

2 teaspoons kosher salt

1 teaspoon freshly ground black pepper

1 tablespoon chopped fresh oregano

1 tablespoon chopped fresh rosemary

1 tablespoon chopped fresh thyme

PIZZA DOUGH

1¼ cups warm water (105–110°F)

1¼ teaspoons sugar

1 packet yeast

1 tablespoon kosher salt

3 cups all-purpose flour

Pizza Sauce:

1. Place the olive oil in a saucepan over medium-low heat. Add the garlic and shallot and simmer slowly for a few minutes, until the oil becomes infused with their flavors. Add the can of tomatoes with their juices. Add the salt and black pepper. Add the fresh oregano, rosemary, and thyme and stir to combine.

2. Raise the heat to high and bring the mixture to a boil. When it boils, turn off the heat.

3. Use an immersion blender to break up the tomatoes, or carefully transfer the sauce to a blender or food processor and process briefly.

Pizza Dough:

4. Combine the warm water and sugar. Add the packet of yeast and stir. Add 1 tablespoon of kosher salt.

5. Place the flour in a food processor fitted with a dough blade. Pulse it briefly.

6. With the processor running, slowly add the yeast mixture. Note that you might not need all of the liquid. The dough will start to form into a ball. After the ball forms, let the machine knead the dough for another minute or so.

PIZZA TOPPINGS

Fresh mozzarella cheese

1 teaspoon dried oregano leaves

Kosher salt, to taste

Freshly ground black pepper, to taste

1 tablespoon extra-virgin olive oil

Parmagiano-Reggiano cheese

7. Transfer the dough to a lightly-floured surface. Shape the dough into a round ball by turning it in upon itself. Close off the bottom seam by twisting the dough to seal.

8. Add the 1 tablespoon olive oil to a bowl and spin the dough in the oil to coat it evenly. Cover the dough with plastic wrap and place it someplace warm to rise for 1 to 2 hours. The dough can also be refrigerated overnight and allowed to rise for about an hour the next day before baking.

9. Preheat the oven (with a pizza stone in the oven) to 450°F.

10. For one pizza, break off a piece of the pizza dough, roughly the size of a softball. Work and roll the dough on a lightly floured surface with your hands and a rolling pin to about ¼ inch thick. Be sure to keep the shape round. If you're adventurous, try tossing the dough in the air and catching it on your knuckles to stretch it out.

11. Form a crust by pressing a lip around the edges. Place the dough on the heated pizza stone.

12. Add a light coating of the tomato sauce to the dough. Add desired toppings, such as applewood smoked bacon and red onions or bell peppers. Be creative.

13. Top the pizza with some mozzarella, dried oregano, salt, and pepper. Drizzle with the olive oil (this will aid in the cooking of any raw ingredients) and grate some fresh Parmagiano-Reggiano cheese on top.

14. Cook the pizza until the crust is golden brown and the cheese is melted, 6 to 10 minutes.

FLOUR TORTILLAS

PREP TIME: 5 MINUTES | CHILL & COOK TIME: 37 MINUTES | READY IN: 42 MINUTES

Learn how easy it is to make your own homemade flour tortillas. Those store-bought lifeless, undercooked, prepackaged tortillas can't hold a candle to these. I like to make extra dough; then freeze it for another time. It only takes a few minutes to have a griddle perfect flour tortilla on the table when you prepare them ahead of time.

MAKES 6 SERVINGS

4 cups all-purpose flour
1½ tablespoons kosher salt
6 tablespoons lard or shortening
3 cups hot water

1. Combine the flour, salt, and lard in a mixing bowl. Mix well to distribute the lard throughout the flour.

2. Add the water a little at a time and stir to start forming the dough, being careful not to overmix.

3. Turn the dough out onto a work surface and, with your hands, begin working the dough into a ball. Work it until it becomes smooth on the outside.

4. Break off small, palm-sized pieces of dough and roll them into balls (golfball-size for 8-inch tortillas).

5. Let them rest on a tray in or out of the refrigerator for 30 minutes. You can freeze them for later at this point.

6. On a floured board, roll each ball out into a round tortilla shape. Cook them on a dry nonstick griddle or in a cast-iron skillet over medium-low heat until brown.

CORN SALSA

PREP TIME: 15 MINUTES | READY IN: 15 MINUTES

MAKES 6 TO 8 SERVINGS

4 ears fresh corn, in their husks

1 red bell pepper, small diced

½ red onion, small diced

⅓ cup chopped fresh cilantro

1 clove garlic, chopped

Zest of 1 lime

Juice of 1 lime

1 tablespoon extra-virgin olive oil

Salt and pepper, to taste

1. Over a hot grill, cook the corn for about 5 minutes, turning when necessary, until the husks are black. Remove from the grill and cool.

2. Husk the corn when cool. With a sharp knife remove the kernels from the cob and place them in a mixing bowl with the remaining ingredients.

3. Mix well and season to taste.

BARBEQUE DRY RUB

PREP TIME: 5 MINUTES | READY IN: 5 MINUTES

MAKES 2¼ CUPS

¼ cup brown sugar

¼ cup sweet paprika

¼ cup kosher salt

3 tablespoons ground black pepper

2 teaspoons garlic powder

2 teaspoons onion powder

1 teaspoon cayenne pepper

1 teaspoon dried basil

1. Place all ingredients in a plastic bag or a container with a tight-fitting lid.

2. Mix well.

Chef's Note: Keep in a sealed container or zip bag to maintain freshness. I usually buy bulk spices on the Internet and make a big batch of this stuff. It will last six months at least.

CHICKEN STOCK

PREP TIME: 10 MINUTES | COOK TIME: 80 MINUTES | READY IN: 90 MINUTES

It's surprisingly easy to make your own homemade chicken stock. As a bonus, you'll have some delicious poached chicken that can be used for chicken salad, chicken burritos, or chicken noodle soup.

MAKES 10 CUPS

4 pounds organic chicken pieces, with bones

2 stalks celery, coarsely chopped

2 carrots, peeled and coarsely chopped

1 organic white onion, halved

3 bay leaves

Several black peppercorns

10 cups cold water

1. Place the chicken, celery, carrots, onion, bay leaves, and peppercorns in a large pot. Add the cold water, enough to cover.

2. Simmer over low heat for 1 hour, removing the chicken breasts after 20 minutes of simmering. Leave the bones in the mixture. At the end of the hour, drain the stock (for a very clear stock, line the strainer with cheesecloth). Cool briefly before refrigerating or freezing.

3. Refrigerate the chicken breast for use in other recipes.

HARVEST EATING SEASONING

PREPARATION TIME: 5 MINUTES | READY IN: 5 MINUTES

This seasoning is great on a number of dishes and, I use throughout the book. It's a catch-all seasoning that I created to spice up my cooking.

MAKES ¼ CUP

2 tablespoons salt

1½ tablespoons black pepper

1 teaspoon garlic powder

½ tablespoon dried oregano

½ teaspoon dried thyme

¼ teaspoon ground cumin

Combine all the ingredients in a small tuppeware container. Put the lid on it and give it a shake.

Chef's Note: This will keep for months in a sealed container. It can be used on fish, chicken, beef, eggs, and with any other number of recipes.

BOLOGNESE SAUCE

PREP TIME: 20 MINUTES | COOK TIME: 45 MINUTES | READY IN: 65 MINUTES

The classic Italian meat sauce bolognese is a thick, hearty, and very flavorful ragù that is a staple of northern Italy's Bolgna region. The use of two meats, wine, herbs, and cream make this a very hearty recipe. It's tremendously satisfying with homemade pasta, crisp bread, and good red wine.

MAKES 6 SERVINGS

3½ to 4 tablespoons olive oil, divided

½ cup diced celery

½ cup diced carrot

½ cup diced Spanish onion

Kosher salt, to taste

Freshly ground black pepper, to taste

1 pound ground pork

1 pound ground beef (chuck)

½ cup Italian red wine

1 (28-ounce) can organic Italian plum tomatoes

1 bunch fresh thyme, chopped

1 bunch fresh oregano, chopped

2 garlic cloves, minced

¼ cup organic heavy cream

½ cup extra-virgin olive oil

¼ cup Parmigiano-Reggiano cheese

1. In a heavy-bottomed pot with a tight-fitting lid, heat 3 tablespoons of the olive oil over medium heat. Add the celery, carrot, onion, salt, and pepper and sauté for 5 minutes.

2. Add the ground meats and ½ to 1 tablespoon more oil. Season again with more salt and pepper. Cook the meat, stirring often, about 10 minutes or until no pink remains.

3. Deglaze the pan with the wine. Add the tomatoes, thyme, oregano, garlic, cream, and olive oil and cover tightly. Reduce the heat to low and cook for 30 minutes. After 30 minutes, break up any remaining large pieces of tomatoes.

4. Add the cheese, adjust the seasoning and continue simmering, uncovered, for another 15 minutes to allow excess moisture to evaporate.

Chef's Note: You can add some additional extra-virgin olive oil on top when serving. This sauce goes best with wide noodles or shells that will hold the thick sauce. Look for papparadelle, a flat, long, wide noodle with rippled edges.

CRÈME FRÂICHE

PREP TIME: I MINUTE | FERMENTING TIME: 24 HOURS | READY IN: 24 HOURS

Crème frâiche is a cultured dessert cream that also can be used in savory dishes. This is historically a French specialty that was discovered because fresh cream would naturally culture without refrigeration in ancient France. This is always in our fridge. My daughters love it with dates and fig jam. It is very simple to make.

MAKES I CUP

8 ounces organic heavy cream

2 tablespoons organic buttermilk

1. Whisk together the cream and buttermilk in a small bowl. Cover the bowl with plastic wrap.

2. Allow to rest someplace warm (70 to 80°F) for 24 hours. A kitchen counter or a sunny window works great. If your house is cooler than 70 degrees it may take a little longer. It will be done when it is the texture of yogurt.

3. Then refrigerate the mixture until it becomes cold and thickened.

Chef's Note: This is the best topping for fruit, assorted desserts, cereal, and many other things. Avoid creams that contain gums like guar or carrageenan gum.

BROWN SAUCE

PREP TIME: 1 HOUR | COOK TIME: 4½ HOURS | READY IN: 5½ HOURS

MAKES 2 CUPS

3 pieces veal bones

¼ cup tomato paste

1 onion, quartered

1 garlic bulb, halved

2 ribs celery, cut into 1-inch chunks

2 carrots, cut into 1-inch chunks

1 cup red wine

2½ quarts water

2 bay leaves

1 bunch fresh thyme

10 black peppercorns

3 tablespoons butter, softened

3 tablespoons all-purpose flour

1. Preheat the oven to 350°F. Cook the bones in a roasting pan for about 1 hour or until brown.

2. Add the tomato paste and vegetables and continue to cook for an additional 20 minutes. Add the wine and deglaze the pan by scraping up any bits of meat.

3. Transfer the mixture to a large stock pot and add the water, bay leaves, thyme, and peppercorns.

4. Bring the stock to a simmer over low heat. Cook for about 4 hours or until the flavor is desirable.

5. In a bowl mix the butter and flour until smooth. Add this to the stock while whisking.

6. Cook the sauce for an additional 10 minutes. Strain and serve over your favorite cut of beef.

HARVEST EATING TOMATO SAUCE

My version of a classic Italian style red sauce or ragù, which can be used on pasta, pizza, or any other Italian recipe calling for a red sauce or gravy, is made with imported San Marzano tomatoes. If you can't find these, any canned organic tomato will do. The infusion of the oil with herbs and garlic really brings the thunder.

MAKES 6 SERVINGS

¼ cup extra-virgin olive oil

¼ cup minced onion

6 garlic cloves, sliced

1 sprig fresh rosemary

1 sprig fresh thyme

1 (28-ounce) can organic whole peeled tomatoes

Kosher salt, to taste

A few twists of freshly ground black pepper

Dash red pepper flakes (optional)

Dash of heavy cream (optional)

1. Heat the oil in a sauce pot over low heat. Add the onion, garlic, rosemary, and thyme.

2. Simmer slowly for 10 minutes. Place the tomatoes in a food processor or blender and pulse 2 times. Add them to the sauce pot.

3. Season the sauce with the salt and pepper. If you are using the optional red pepper flakes or heavy cream, add them to the sauce. Increase the heat to high and bring the sauce to a boil. After it boils, remove the sauce from the heat. Do not overcook.

HERB BUTTER

PREP TIME: 5 MINUTES | READY IN: 5 MINUTES

Compound butters can bring a lot of flavor to a dish. This is a very simple recipe that I like to make with fresh thyme, rosemary, and parsley. However, it can be made with chives, cilantro, oregano, chervil, or other herbs. Get creative with this recipe.

MAKES 1 CUP

½ pound (2 sticks) fresh local butter

3 tablespoons chopped fresh herbs

Pinch of gray sea salt

A few twists of black pepper

1. Soften the butter at room temperature or heat in a double boiler over low heat until just soft; do not melt. Add the herbs, salt, and pepper; mix well.

2. Wrap the butter in parchment paper or waxed paper to form a log. It can last in the freezer for about two months or in the refrigerator for about one week.

BASIL-GARLIC PARMESAN BUTTER

PREP TIME: 5 MINUTES | READY IN: 5 MINUTES

This delicious flavored butter is a cinch to make and tastes great on many dishes, including seared filet mignon, grilled local corn, or a baked potato.

MAKES ½ CUP

¼ pound (1 stick) organic unsalted butter

3 tablespoons freshly grated Parmigiano-Reggiano cheese

1 teaspoon garlic powder

1 tablespoon minced fresh basil

Freshly ground black pepper, to taste

1. Put the stick of butter in a bowl and let it come to room temperature; do not microwave!

2. Add the cheese, garlic powder, basil, and pepper. Mix well with a fork or wooden spoon.

3. Wrap the butter in parchment paper or waxed paper to form a log. It can last in the freezer for about two months or in the refrigerator for about one week.

Chef's Note: Use on fresh corn, cooked pasta, toasted bread, or any steamed vegetables.

SAUCE BÉCHAMEL

PREP TIME: 5 MINUTES | COOK TIME: 15 MINUTES | READY IN: 20 MINUTES

This classic "mother sauce" is one of the five foundational sauces in French cuisine. It can be used in many ways and in many variations. It's a perfect addition on steamed vegetables, on a ham sandwich, or in a lasagna.

MAKES 4 CUPS

½ cup all-purpose flour

¼ pound (1 stick) organic unsalted butter

3 cups organic whole milk

2 whole cloves

1 bay leaf

½ organic white onion

Kosher salt, to taste

A few twists of black pepper

1. Place the flour and the butter in a sauce pot over low heat. Stir for about 5 minutes. Do not brown the flour.

2. Add the milk and whisk to combine. Stick the cloves through the bay leaf into the onion half and add it to the milk mixture.

3. Season the mixture to taste with the salt and pepper and then bring it to a simmer and cook until the sauce is thick enough to coat the back of a spoon.

Chef's Note: The addition of two cups of shredded Gruyére cheese melted in this sauce will result in Mornay Sauce, which is great for dishes such as macaroni and cheese or steamed vegetables.

VELOUTÉ SAUCE

PREP TIME: 5 MINUTES | COOK TIME: 15 MINUTES | READY IN: 20 MINUTES

One of the five classic French mother sauces, this sauce can become the hearty core of many recipes, including the Harvest Eating chicken pot pie.

MAKES 5 CUPS

¼ pound (1 stick) organic butter

¼ cup all-purpose flour

5 cups organic chicken stock

Harvest Eating House Seasoning (page 278)

1. Melt the butter in a saucepan over low heat. Add the flour and whisk to make a roux. Remove it from the heat and add the chicken stock, whisking slowly to combine.

2. The mixture should thicken slightly. Add a pinch of Harvest Eating House Seasoning. Add more stock as necessary to achieve the desired consistency.

CUMIN-CILANTRO CREMA

PREP TIME: 3 MINUTES | READY IN: 3 MINUTES

This is a simple recipe for a flavored crema *(Italian for cream) to use in a variety of recipes. It's quite nice on burritos, quesadillas, or a grilled piece of fish.*

MAKES ⅔ CUP

½ cup organic sour cream or homemade Crème Fraîche (page 280)

2 tablespoons chopped fresh cilantro

1 tablespoon freshly squeezed lime juice

1 teaspoon ground cumin

1. Combine the sour cream, cilantro, lime juice, and cumin in a bowl.

2. Mix with a wire whisk until well combined.

HORSERADISH CREAM SAUCE

PREP TIME: 2 MINUTES | READY IN: 2 MINUTES

Here is a delicious sauce to serve with prime rib, roast beef, or steak. I use thick Greek yogurt instead of sour cream in order to get a tangy flavor. Use plenty of horseradish for flavor, grating your own fresh horseradish root if it is available.

MAKES 6 SERVINGS

3 tablespoons prepared horseradish

½ cup Greek yogurt

Pinch of kosher salt

Pinch of freshly ground black pepper

1. Combine the horseradish, yogurt, salt, and pepper in a bowl.

2. Whisk until well combined.

WASABI VINAIGRETTE

PREP TIME: 5 MINUTES | READY IN: 5 MINUTES

The very nice Asian flavors in this vinaigrette are reminiscent of trips to the sushi bar. This is perfect on a piece of seared summer tuna. On Cape Cod, where we vacation each summer, fresh local tuna is abundant, and this is the vinaigrette I like to serve with it.

MAKES 2 CUPS

⅔ cup pure olive oil

2 teaspoon wasabi powder

1 teaspoon minced fresh ginger

2 tablespoons rice wine vinegar

1 tablespoon toasted sesame oil

1 tablespoon low-sodium soy sauce

1 small handful fresh cilantro (¼ cup)

Kosher salt, to taste

Freshly ground black pepper, to taste

1. Combine the olive oil, wasabi powder, ginger, vinegar, sesame oil, soy sauce, and cilantro in a blender or jar with a tight-fitting lid.

2. Process in the blender at high speed, or shake the jar vigorously, until the vinaigrette is emulsified.

3. If the mixture is too thick, add more vinegar, 1 tablespoon at a time.

4. Season with salt and pepper. If storing, shake to re-blend before using.

CARAMEL SAUCE

This is a simple and delicious sauce that is easy to make and keeps well in the refrigerator. Real caramel sauce does not contain preservatives or stabilizers. This sauce is tremendous when used on ice cream, bananas, or brownies.

MAKES 2 SERVINGS

1 cup granulated sugar

1 teaspoon corn syrup

2 tablespoons water

½ pint organic heavy cream

1. Combine the sugar, corn syrup, and water in a stainless steel sauce pot over medium-high heat. Bring to a boil.

2. Cook until the mixture starts to change color. Whisk often while cooking. When the mixture becomes a dark mahogany color, add the cream whisking to combine. Remove from the heat.

3. Cool to room temperature, then transfer it to a jar and store it in the refrigerator.

....

Chef's Note: This mixture becomes extremely hot. Make sure children are not present when you are cooking it. This dish should *not* be left unattended. Be very careful!

....

GANACHE

PREP TIME: 5 MINUTES | COOK TIME: 15 MINUTES | READY IN: 20 MINUTES

Ganache could not be simpler to make and brings the wow *factor to many desserts. Starting with high-quality chocolate and the best heavy cream you can find will make this sauce perfect.*

MAKES 2 CUPS

7 ounces high-quality dark chocolate

1 cup organic heavy cream

1. Cut the chocolate into small pieces with a serrated knife and place them in a heatproof work bowl.

2. Bring the cream to just under boiling ("scalding") over medium-high heat, being careful not to let it boil.

3. Pour the hot cream into the bowl and stir to melt the chocolate.

PASTRY DOUGH (PÂTE BRISÉE)

PREP TIME: 15 MINUTES | READY IN: 15 MINUTES

This surprisingly easy pastry or pie dough is also known as a pâte brisée. The trick is not overworking the dough lest it become tough. If making a sweet pie dough, use two tablespoons of sugar instead of the salt.

MAKES 1 (10-INCH) PIE

2½ cups all-purpose flour

1 tablespoon kosher salt

½ pound (2 sticks) butter, chilled and chopped into half-inch cubes

1 cup ice cold water

1. Add the salt and flour to the bowl of a food processor fitted with a dough blade. Pulse to mix. Add the butter. Pulse until the butter resembles small pebbles. Be careful not to overwork the dough.

2. While pulsing, add the water to the flour and butter mixture. Process until the mixture just starts to come together.

3. Transfer the dough to a cold, hard surface. Working quickly and using extra flour as needed, mold by hand into a flat disc. Wrap the disc in plastic wrap and refrigerate a minimum of 45 minutes.

CANNING & PRESERVING

THERE ARE ALL KINDS OF NIFTY gadgets and tools out there to help you with your canning adventures. If you are someone who likes great tools at a good price then look for the Presto pressure canner. Not only is it a quality device, it's reasonably priced and doubles as a water-bath canner for foods that do not require high pressure. I have used one many, many times with great success. Pressure canners are good to have if you plan on canning often, and they are required to process low-acid foods like vegetables and meat, but they are not necessary to get started with simple water-bath canning. You may already have all the tools you need at home. You will need mason jars with lids and rings. Be sure to always use new lids and rings every time to start the process. You cannot reuse the lids, and the rings will rust quickly so just replace them. Most stores that sell mason jars sell the lids and rings separately which is great if you have jars already. Or you can go to www.canningpantry.com to order new ones. Also, most grocery stores are now carrying these supplies as canning is gaining in popularity. Be sure to buy them early in spring because the stores sell out and only get replacement stock a few times per year.

A great website for avid canners is www.freshpreserving.com. It has loads of how-to information, recipes, and new product information. It also features a busy discussion forum for canners looking to share knowledge and get inspired from other experienced home canning enthusiasts. I also recommend that every home canner own the *Ball Blue Book*; it is the canners bible.

For basic water-bath canning you will need a pot large enough to fit your jar or jars inside (they cannot be touching) with about five to six inches of space above to allow for the water to cover and room for it to boil. You will need a round stainless steel rack to fit in the bottom of the pot as the jars cannot be resting on the pot itself. The direct heat will cause them to break. Finally, you need a canning funnel and pair of large, sturdy canning tongs for removing the jars. Please do not attempt to remove jars with standard kitchen tongs, trust me, it's easy to get badly burned when the jar plops back into boiling water. *Buy canning tongs*!

Before you ever eat anything you have preserved yourself, always check the lid to make sure it is securely attached. *Do not eat* anything from a jar with a loose lid.

APPLESAUCE IN JARS

PREP TIME: 10 MINUTES | COOKING TIME: 60 MINUTE | TOTAL TIME: 70 MINUTES

MAKES ABOUT 8
(16-OUNCE) JARS

12 pounds apples, peeled, cored,
quartered and drained

Water

3 cups organic raw sugar

4 tablespoons lemon juice

¼ teaspoon ground cinnamon

¼ teaspoon ground cloves

8 (16-ounce) glass preserving jars
with lids and bands

1. Fill a pot with enough water to cover the jars by at least three inches. Put the rack in the bottom. Bring the water to a boil over high heat. Sterilize the empty jars and lids by boiling them for at least 1 minute. Remove them with canning tongs to a clean work surface.

2. Combine the apples with enough water to almost cover the apples) in a large stainless steel saucepan. Bring to a boil over medium heat. Reduce the heat and boil gently, stirring occasionally, for 5 to 10 minutes, until the apples are tender Remove from the heat and let cool slightly, about 10 minutes.

3. Purée the apples in a food mill or a food processor fitted with a metal blade until smooth.

4. Return the apple purée to the stainless steel pot. Add the raw sugar, lemon juice, cinnamon, and clove. Bring to a boil over medium heat, stirring frequently to prevent sticking.

5. Spoon the hot applesauce into the sterilized jars leaving ½ inch of space at the top. Remove any air bubbles by gently tapping the sides of the jars. Wipe the rims clean. Place the lids on the jars and screw on the band.

6. Place the filled jars on the rack inside the pot of water. Bring the water to a rapid boil.

7. Boil the jars for 20 minutes, adjusting for altitude.

8. Transfer the jars with the tongs to a cutting board or trivet. While cooling, the lids of the jar will pop as the air is removed in the process. Check the lids for a good seal after 24 hours.

CANNED TOMATOES

PREP TIME: 10 MINUTES | COOKING TIME: 60 MINUTES | TOTAL TIME: 70 MINUTES

MAKES ABOUT 12 QUARTS

10 pounds fresh tomatoes

1 teaspoon salt

1 teaspoon lemon juice

1. Core the tomatoes and score an X on two sides. Place them in boiling water for 20 seconds and transfer to ice water to "shock" them. Remove the skins when cool to the touch.

2. Combine the skinned tomatoes, salt, and lemon juice in a large bowl.

3. Fill the pot with enough water to cover the jars by at least three inches. Put the rack in the bottom. Bring the water to a boil over high heat. Sterilize the empty jars and lids by boiling them for at least 1 minute. Remove them with canning tongs to a clean work surface.

4. Fill the jars with the tomatoes and wipe the rims clean. (This is important to ensure a good seal.) Place the lids on the jars and screw on the bands.

5. Place the filled jars on the rack inside the pot of water. Bring the water to a rapid boil.

6. Boil the jars for 30 minutes, adjusting for altitude.

7. Transfer the jars with the tongs to a cutting board or trivet. While cooling, the lids of the jar will pop as the air is removed in the process. This means your jars are properly sealed. Check the lids for a good seal after 24 hours. The lids should not flex up and down when the center is pressed.

TOMATILLO SALSA

PREP TIME: 10 MINUTES | COOKING TIME: 60 MINUTES | TOTAL TIME: 70 MINUTES

MAKES ABOUT 12 QUARTS

6 tomatillos, chopped

6 large tomatoes, chopped

3 large white onions, chopped

1 red bell pepper, chopped

1 green bell peppers, chopped

1 yellow bell pepper, chopped

2 whole jalapeños, chopped

1 whole chipotle, chopped

8 teaspoons salt

½ cup red wine vinegar

1 garlic clove, chopped

juice of one lime

2 ancho chiles, chopped

1. Combine all ingredients in a large stock pot and bring to a boil.

2. Fill the pot with enough water to cover the jars by at least three inches. Put the rack in the bottom. Bring the water to a boil over high heat. Sterilize the empty jars and lids by boiling them for at least 1 minute. Remove them with the tongs to a clean work surface.

3. Fill the jars with the hot salsa and wipe the rims clean. Place the lids on the jars and screw on the bands.

4. Place the filled jars on the rack inside the pot of water. Bring the water to a rapid boil.

5. Boil the jars for 15 minutes, adjusting for altitude.

6. Transfer the jars with the tongs to a cutting board or trivet. While cooling, the lids of the jar will pop as the air is removed in the process. This means your jars are properly sealed. Check the lids for a good seal after 24 hours. The lids should not flex up and down when the center is pressed.

PICKLED GREEN BEANS

PREP TIME: 10 MINUTES | COOKING TIME: 60 MINUTES | TOTAL TIME: 70 MINUTES

MAKES 6 PINTS

1 cup water

2 cups white wine vinegar

1 cup sugar

2 pounds green beans, cleaned and trimmed

2 shallots, chopped

1. Combine the water, vinegar, and sugar in a large pot over medium-high heat.

2. When the water comes to a boil, add the green beans and shallots and cook for 5 minutes over medium heat.

3. Fill a large pot with enough water to cover the mason jars by at least three inches. Put a rack in the bottom. Bring the water to a boil over high heat. Sterilize the empty jars and lids by boiling them for at least 1 minute. Remove them with canning tongs to a clean work surface.

4. Fill the jars with the beans and wipe the rims clean. Place the lids on the jars and screw on the bands.

5. Place the filled jars on the rack inside the pot of water. Bring the water to a rapid boil.

6. Boil the jars for 30 minutes, adjusting for altitude.

7. Transfer the jars with the tongs to a cutting board or trivet. While cooling, the lids of the jar will pop as the air is removed in the process. This means your jars are properly sealed. Check the lids for a good seal after 24 hours. The lids should not flex up and down when the center is pressed.

EXTREME
COOKONOMOMICS

I N RECENT YEARS THE AMOUNT OF people moving back to the country has increased exponentially. A "ruralpolitan" according to *Consumer Reports* is "a professional who has abandoned the urban dwelling for a rural lifestyle and lives on three acres or more, typically within forty miles of a city." People like me are deciding that country living has major advantages in quality of life and recreational opportunities. Having a little land affords many activities that can relate to food production as well. When I decided in 2002 that I wanted my family to have access to fresh air and land, we bought our farm in Western North Carolina. The first thing we did was start our garden. We decided on a row garden that produced many of our foods. In addition to gardening we had chickens for eggs, goats for milk, and were very close to buying a Jersey cow as well. To be honest, the Jersey cow is something I still would like to have. Extreme cookonomics is best suited to people who have access to some land, although it does not have to be a big parcel. Recently, there has been a growing trend which is directly opposite of the ruralpolitans. These are urban farmers who are raising chickens and goats within the city limits of many major cities for eggs and milk.

Recently in Denver a gentleman was profiled in a newspaper story about his backyard chicken coop. He lives on a quarter of an acre. Many cities are fine with this as long as there are no roosters around, for obvious reasons. His neighbors don't mind as he provides them with fresh eggs.

Some activities I would consider as extreme cookonomics would be keeping goats, chickens, cows, sheep, lambs, and bees. These creatures can produce the raw materials for many exciting high-quality foods. Keeping animals like these is very rewarding but does take time and money, however the products you make can help offset the cost investment. See the Cookonomics section of HarvestEating.com for a resource list.

∽ A HARVEST-EATING PANTRY ∽

I RECENTLY HEARD THE TERM "NEW normal." So many things we do are normal: "we normally get pizza delivered every Saturday night." New normal is about redefining what we normally do. When we roll through the grocery store we tend to shop for foods we normally buy without thinking about their health or environmental impacts. So a *new normal* would be to say, "lets make pizza tonight with the tomatoes we canned and the cheese we made and the sausage we ground." Eating what you grow is best, eating organic is better. So the next time you pick up that basket or push the cart , start a *new normal* for yourself by selecting items that are unprocessed, organic, and natural.

You may be thinking, "that's great if you have the time to clean and cook sixteen artichokes for your dip, but I have to go to work, drop the kids off at soccer practice, go to the bank, and pay the bills." Sometimes it is necessary to get processed, after all we don't have all the time our ancestors had, or the skills. It's okay to buy packaged foods when you need to, but just try to shop smartly and buy organic as much as possible. When you go to the grocery store and you want something sweet like a bag of cookies, do this: buy the ingredients instead. Then make them with the ones you love, and I guarantee those will be the best cookies you've ever had and not just for the flavor.

STOCKING A HARVEST
～ EATING PANTRY AND FRIDGE ～

K EEPING A WELL STOCKED PANTRY is the key to any style of cookery. It takes some basic organizational techniques like keeping an inventory list and a handy note pad to place items on that are getting low. I try to maintain an inventory of commonly used items and put them on the grocery list when they get below two. The pantry items include staple items that need to be stored in your refrigerator.

STOCKING YOUR PANTRY AND FRIDGE

BAKING

Almond extract

Baking powder

Baking soda

Brown sugar, light
and dark

Chocolate, 62% & 70%
cacao Sharrfenberger

Coconut milk

Corn meal, locally stone-
ground

Cornstarch

Flour, whole wheat,
bread, and all purpose
(King Arthur)

Honey, several varieties
of local

Lard

Lemon oil

Organic unsweetened
coconut flakes

Sugar, confectioners'
and superfine

Vanilla extract

Yeast

CANNED GOODS

Assorted mustards

Assorted hot sauces

Canned beans, black,
pinto, white, kidney

Capers

Chipotles in adobo

Garbanzo beans

Olives, black and green

San Marzano tomatoes

Tomato paste

**DRY GOODS
(SUNDRIES)**

Assorted Dried chilies
(de Arbol, New Mexi-
can red chilies, pe-
quín, ancho, chipotle)

Fruits, dried (apricots,
raisins, figs, cherries)

Herbs, freshly grown
(container garden in
the winter and a
kitchen garden in
the spring)

Kosher salt

Mushrooms, dried
(porcini, shiitake,
morel, chanterelle, etc.)

Nuts (almonds, peanuts,
hazelnuts, cashews,
pine nuts, walnuts)

Oils (extra-virgin olive oil,
pure olive oil, olive oil,
coconut oil, truffle oil,
toasted sesame oil)

Pastas (ziti, farfalle, linguini, shells, lasagna,
etc.)

Spices, whole spices
(coriander, cloves,
nutmeg, allspice,
peppercorns, etc.);
for a complete list of
spices go to Har-
vesteating.com

Vinegars (red wine, white
wine, cider, balsamic,
rice wine, sherry, white)

STOCKS

Chicken stock

Veal stock

Vegetable stock

MEATS & DAIRY

Bacon

Hard cured salami

Salt pork

Butter

Cheddar cheese

Cream

Eggs

Fresh mozzerella

Milk

Parmesan cheese

Yogurt

PRODUCE

Apples

Bananas

Carrots

Celery

Citrus

Garlic

Potatoes

Onions

Shallots

INDEX